Prairie Falcon Monitoring Protocol for Pinnacles National Monument

Narrative - Version 2.3

Natural Resource Report NPS/SFAN/NRR—2011/466

Gavin Emmons
Jim Petterson
National Park Service
Pinnacles National Monument
Research and Resource Management
5000 Highway 146
Paicines, CA 95043

Marcus Koenen
David Press
National Park Service
Golden Gate National Recreation Area
Fort Cronkhite, Bldg 1063
Sausalito, CA 94965

November 2011

U.S. Department of the Interior
National Park Service
Natural Resource Stewardship and Science
Fort Collins, Colorado

The National Park Service, Natural Resource Stewardship and Science office in Fort Collins, Colorado publishes a range of reports that address natural resource topics of interest and applicability to a broad audience in the National Park Service and others in natural resource management, including scientists, conservation and environmental constituencies, and the public.

The Natural Resource Report Series is used to disseminate results of scientific studies in the physical, biological, and social sciences for both the advancement of science and the achievement of the National Park Service mission. The series provides contributors with a forum for displaying comprehensive data that are often deleted from journals because of page limitations.

All manuscripts in the series receive the appropriate level of peer review to ensure that the information is scientifically credible, technically accurate, appropriately written for the intended audience, and designed and published in a professional manner. This report received formal, high-level peer review based on the importance of its content, or its potentially controversial or precedent-setting nature. Peer review was conducted by highly qualified individuals with subject area technical expertise and was overseen by a peer review manager.

Views, statements, findings, conclusions, recommendations, and data in this report do not necessarily reflect views and policies of the National Park Service, U.S. Department of the Interior. Mention of trade names or commercial products does not constitute endorsement or recommendation for use by the U.S. Government.

This report is available from the San Francisco Bay Area Network Inventory and Monitoring Program (http://science.nature.nps.gov/im/units/sfan/index.cfm) and the Natural Resource Publications Management website (http://www.nature.nps.gov/publications/nrpm/).

Please cite this publication as:

Emmons, G., J. Petterson, M. Koenen, and D. Press. 2011. Prairie falcon monitoring protocol for Pinnacles National Monument: narrative - version 2.3. Natural Resource Report NPS/SFAN/NRR—2011/466. National Park Service, Fort Collins, Colorado.

NPS 114/111562, November 2011

Revision History Log

Prev. Version #	Revision Date	Author	Changes Made	Reason for Change	New Version #
NA	Sept. 26, 2003	G. Emmons, A. Fesnock	1st draft sent for review		NA
NA	June 2005	G. Emmons, A. Fesnock.	Refined and augmented contents	Respond to internal review	1.02
1.02	May 2008	G. Emmons, D. Press, J. Pettersen, M. Koenen	Clarifications, largely to data analysis section	Respond to peer-review comments	1.1
1.1	May 2009	M. Koenen, G. Emmons, P. Johnson, D. Adams	Clarifications, largely to data analysis; inclusion of SOPs in main document	Respond to peer-review comments	2.1
2.1	Mar 2010	M. Koenen	Added final changes to sampling design and data analysis	To incorporate findings from Starcevich and Steinhorst (2010)	2.2
2.2	June 2011	D. Adams, D. Roberts	Made title change corrections on p.ii, 20, and 27.	Respond to request from P. Latham, PWR I&M Prgm Mgr.	2.3

CONTENTS

CONTENTS (continued)

CONTENTS (continued)

Figures

Tables

Appendixes

Executive Summary

This protocol and the attached standard operating procedures (SOP) detail the background, field methods, data management, annual and long-term reporting and analyses, and operational requirements to monitor prairie falcons (*Falco mexicanus*) at Pinnacles National Monument in California. Prairie falcons nesting at the monument are sensitive to human disturbances from climbing and hiking activities.

Raptor monitoring began in 1984 with the negotiated settlement of a potential lawsuit. The lawsuit was threatened as a result of the monument's desire to close off parts of the park including popular climbing routes to reduce access to breeding prairie falcon areas. The compromise negotiated required the park to monitor cliff nesting raptors annually to track breeding behavior and establish climbing advisories only in those areas where falcon nesting activity occurs. This has been largely perceived as a win-win by both the monument and the climbing community.

Initially, raptor monitoring focused on minimizing disturbance in areas regularly visited by climbers (core areas). As time allowed, monitoring was also conducted in areas less accessible to the public (non-core areas). Expanding the monitoring area has allowed the park to evaluate long-term changes in population and fecundity. The monitoring described in this protocol is focused on the following objectives:

1. Track changes in prairie falcon occupancy for all historically occupied territories.

2. Track changes in prairie falcon fecundity success as measured by a. number of chicks/nest produced and b. number of chicks/nest fledged in historically occupied areas.

The field season begins in January with the onset of the nesting season. The last nestlings typically fledge by mid July. Field surveys are conducted by one technician throughout the nesting surveys. All historic territories are visited a maximum of three times to determine occupancy. Territories are monitored up to 4 hours per visit to observe territorial behaviors such as defensive territorial displays, food exchanges between males and females, use of perches or night roosts. To determine fecundity, nests are visited frequently enough to positively identify nesting stage including territorial occupancy, courtship, incubation, rearing of nestlings, and fledging of young within a breeding season.

Climbing advisories are posted at the beginning of the breeding season to restrict access to areas historically used by cliff nesting raptors. The advisories are lifted if there is no territorial cliff nesting raptor or when activity around a nest ceases (i.e., nest failed or chicks fledged).

To date, more than 20 years of data show a relatively stable population in the monument. From 1984 – 2009 there have been an average of 7.4 territorial pairs in the core area. There have been an average of 6.3 nesting pairs producing 19.3 nestlings per year. The number of fledglings per nest have ranged from 0 to 4.4 per year. Including all territories, the most nestlings were produced in 1994 (45) and the second most in 2009 (41). No nestlings were produced in 1998 during a year of heavy rains which likely prevented nesting.

Ancillary data collected during the field investigations have helped document two other cliff nesting raptors (golden eagles [*Aquila chrysaetus*] and peregrine falcons [*Falco peregrinus*]). Five other raptors have been documented at the park including: American Kestrel (*Falco sparverius*), Cooper's Hawk (*Accipiter cooperii*), Red-shouldered Hawk (*Buteo lineatus*), Red-tailed Hawk (*Buteo jamaicensis*), and White Tailed Kite (*Elanus leucurus*). Documented owl species include Barn Owl (*Tyto alba*), Great Horned Owl (*Bubo virginianus*), Northern Pygmy Owl (*Glaucidium californicum*), and Western Screech Owl (*Megascops kennicottii*). The monument has been involved with the Condor Recovery Program since 2003. There are now more than 26 California Condors (*Gymnogyps californianus*) in the monument. In 2010, the first condors nested in the monument in over 100 years.

Acknowledgements

Previous versions of this protocol were written by Gavin Emmons (Raptor Biotech) and parts by Amy Fesnock (previous Wildlife Biologist of Pinnacles National Monument). Guidance during the protocol development was provided by Jim Petterson, Wildlife Biologist, Pinnacles National Monument. Jason Herynk developed a state of the art Microsoft Access database, which was improved by Dave Press. Stephen Skartvedt provided GIS support. Andrea Williams provided comments to an earlier draft of this protocol. Dawn Adams and Kris Freeman provided technical editing assistance. Drs. Gretchen LeBuhn and Ed Connor provided comments to an earlier version of this document. Drs. Leigh Ann Starcevich and Kirk Steinhorst provided assistance with a power analysis, overall sampling design, and data analyses sections.

Acronyms

AARWP	Annual Administrative Report and Work Plan
ANOVA	Analysis of variance
CDFG	California Department of Fish and Game
CNDDB	California Natural Diversity Database
ETA	Estimated time of arrival
FAB	Front-end application builder
FGDC	Federal Geographic Data Committee
FOP	Friends of Pinnacles National Monument
GOGA	Golden Gate National Recreation Area
JSA	Job safety analysis
MANOVA	Multivariate analysis of variance
MS	Microsoft
NPS	National Park Service
NRDT	Natural Resource Database Template
NRPM	Natural Resource Publications Management
PINN	Pinnacles National Monument
PTT	Push to talk
QA/QC	Quality assurance / quality control
RRM	Research and Resource Management
SCPGRG	Santa Cruz Predatory Bird Research Group
SFAN	San Francisco Bay Area Inventory and Monitoring Network
SOTP	Standard operating procedure
UTM	Universal Transverse Mercator
VWS	Ventana Wildlife Society
YOY	Young of the year

1 - Background and Objectives

1.1 Issue Being Addressed and Rationale for Monitoring Raptor Populations

Pinnacles National Monument (PINN) is a National Park Service (NPS) unit located in the Gabilan Mountains of central California, and provides a diverse habitat for cliff-nesting raptor species, including sensitive species such as prairie falcons (*Falco mexicanus*), peregrine falcons (*Falco peregrinus*), and golden eagles (*Aquila chrysaetos*). The park was specifically set aside to protect the rock cliffs and the caves underlying them for the scientific and public interest values, with specific note to not injure or destroy features and wildlife associated with the rocks and caves. Since the founding of the park unit in 1908, the dramatic landscapes, extensive trails, arrays of summits, and cliff-wall routes at PINN have also been used intensively for recreation by rock-climbers and hikers (Rubine 1995).

Raptors are an important component of ecosystems, and their presence at high trophic levels in most food webs make them good indicators of the effects of local and regional changes in ecosystems (Marshall 1957; Newton 1979; Brown 1982; Stiles 1985; Brown et al. 1988; Steenhof 1998; Sodhi et al. 1990; Meyer 1995; Jaksic et al. 1996; Squires and Reynolds 1997; Mazur and James 2000; Haemig 2001; Parrish et al. 2001; Kochert et al. 2002; Roemer et al. 2002; White et al. 2002; Lundberg and Moberg 2003; Croll et al. 2005; Preisser et al. 2005; Sekercioglu 2006a, 2006b). It has been suggested that management activities aimed at preserving habitat for bird populations can have the added benefit of preserving entire ecosystems and their attendant ecosystem services (Mitani et al. 2001; Millenium Ecosystem Assessment 2005). Moreover, raptors have a tremendous following among the public, and many parks provide information on the status and trends of birds in the park through their interpretive programs.

Concerns with nesting raptors being impacted by visitor activities associated with rock climbing and off-trail hiking were identified as early as the 1920's, when the Balconies Cliffs were identified as a "Bird Sanctuary" and visitor use of these cliffs was prohibited (Rechtin 1992). Many scientific studies have documented the negative impacts of human disturbance of raptor nest and roost sites, and the resulting nest failures and territorial abandonment associated with these disturbances. Nesting raptor species at PINN that are sensitive to human disturbance include prairie falcons (Fyfe and Olendorff 1976; Ogden and Hornocker 1977; Harmata et al. 1978; Sitter 1983; Steenhof 1998), peregrine falcons (particularly in remote locations: see Hickey 1942, 1969; Bond 1946; Steenhof 1998), golden eagles (Newton 1979, 1990; Scott 1985; Steidl et al. 1993; Steenhof et al. 1997; Watson 1997; Kochert et al. 1999), sharp-shinned hawks (*Accipiter striatus*; Delannoy and Cruz 1988), and long-eared owls (*Asio otus*; Marks 1986; Marti and Marks 1989; Bloom 1994).

Prairie falcons nest in particularly high numbers at PINN, with an average of 9.6 nesting pairs per year documented from 1984–2006 throughout the park and 6.5 nesting pairs per year documented from 1984–2006 in core areas with historical or potential rock-climbing impacts (Emmons 2006; see Protocol Glossary for terminology definitions related to the raptor monitoring program and Figure 1 for a GIS map of core area locations). Studies of prairie falcon nest occupancy and productivity have also shown the species to be especially sensitive to human disturbance from recreation (Boyce 1982), climbing to nests (Ellis 1973, Kochert et al. 2002), mining (Becker and Ball 1981; Bednarz 1984), agriculture (U.S. Dept. of Interior 1979), habitat

1

destruction and nest site limitation (Becker and Ball 1981; Steenhof et al. 1997), and proximity to major roadways (Platt 1974, Boyce 1982).

The main sources of human disturbance of nesting raptors at PINN are visitors that are rock-climbing and hiking, both on- and off-trail in the park. Scientific studies have consistently suggested that these recreation activities can be balanced against raptor nesting by establishing closure or advisory areas that act as buffers between human activity and raptor nesting during the breeding season (Fyfe and Olendorff 1976; Olsen and Olsen 1978, 1980; Becker and Ball 1981; Suter and Joness 1981; Porter et al. 1987; Holthuijzen et al. 1990; Cade et al. 1996; White et al. 2002).

1.1.1 Historical Development of Breeding Raptor Monitoring in Pinnacles

Raptors have been of interest at PINN since it was established. Park naturalists and local bird enthusiasts have documented nesting raptors since the late 1910s. In the 1970s California Department of Fish and Game (CDFG) conducted a series of surveys assessing habitat used by peregrine and prairie falcons. The Santa Cruz Predatory Bird Research Group (SCPBRG) approached the monument in 1982 with a proposal to assess the impact of climbing on cliff-nesting raptors, and the project was funded and completed in 1984. The recommendation from this project was to continue monitoring breeding success of cliff nesting raptors (specifically prairie falcons and golden eagles; by this time peregrine falcons had been extirpated from PINN).

In 1987, PINN initiated its long-term monitoring program, in part to avoid litigation threatened by visitor access advocates. Monitoring information was used to establish climbing/hiking advisories only around active nests. The climbing/hiking advisories are notices posted at PINN visitor centers and along trails leading to areas with cliff-nesting raptors. These advisories serve to inform hikers and climbers about cliff-nesting raptors and potential disturbances. While they are not forced closures, the advisories reduce potential disturbances by recommending and directing visitors to use other areas within the park. Advisories are lifted when monitoring determines that nesting activity has ceased. This monitoring and management approach represented a win for both managers wishing to protect nesting raptors and a win for climbers wishing access to the park during the peak climbing season.

The field methods set forth in this protocol have been consistently used since 1987. During the early years, however, monitoring focused primarily on "core areas" of the park (Figure 1). "Core areas" include historic territories established in the vicinity of climbing routes. Nest surveys were outside of the core areas (non-core areas) were only conducted as time allowed. Starting in 2000 the park made a commitment to monitor all known historic territories in the park (core and non-core areas).

1.2 Monitoring Questions

The long-term monitoring set out to answer the following questions:
- Are the number of cliff-nesting raptor territories in the highly visited core climbing areas changing over time? Are the numbers changing in the rest of the monument?

- Is productivity of cliff-nesting raptors (number of nestlings per nest that reach fledgling stage) changing over time in the core areas? Is productivity changing in the rest of the monument?

While collecting information on trends, information will be gathered to help the park answer the following management-related question:
- For which areas do climbing advisories need to be established in order to reduce potential disturbance?
- Are there differences in prairie falcon productivity between the core and non-core areas?

If population or productivity trends occur, research could be initiated to address the following question:
- What is causing changes in the number of territories and/or productivity?

1.3 Monitoring Objectives
In order to meet park management objectives to reduce disturbance to nesting raptors and to track population changes over time, this protocol sets forth the following two measurable monitoring objectives:

1. Track changes in prairie falcon occupancy for all historically occupied territories.

2. Track changes in prairie falcon fecundity success as measured by a. number of chicks/nest produced and b. number of chicks/nest fledged in historically occupied territories.

1.4 Management Objectives
Because this protocol grew out of management needs, a clear management objective had been established at the onset of the program. That objective is to protect cliff-nesting raptors from human disturbance by establishing climbing/hiking advisories in core use areas at the beginning of the breeding season (January). These advisories remain in effect until two weeks after the last fledgling occurs (usually mid July). Advisories are also removed in areas where nesting is not confirmed after 3 site visits.

1.5 Other Raptor Species
While not a formal part of this protocol, ancillary data are collected by technicians as they travel through a variety of habitats on the way to and from the prairie falcon sites. During these efforts, for example, technicians gather presence/absence data and productivity for up to 15 other species of raptors (see Appendix D for full list). These data are of great interest to managers because many of these species are considered "species at risk" by the CDFG (2008).

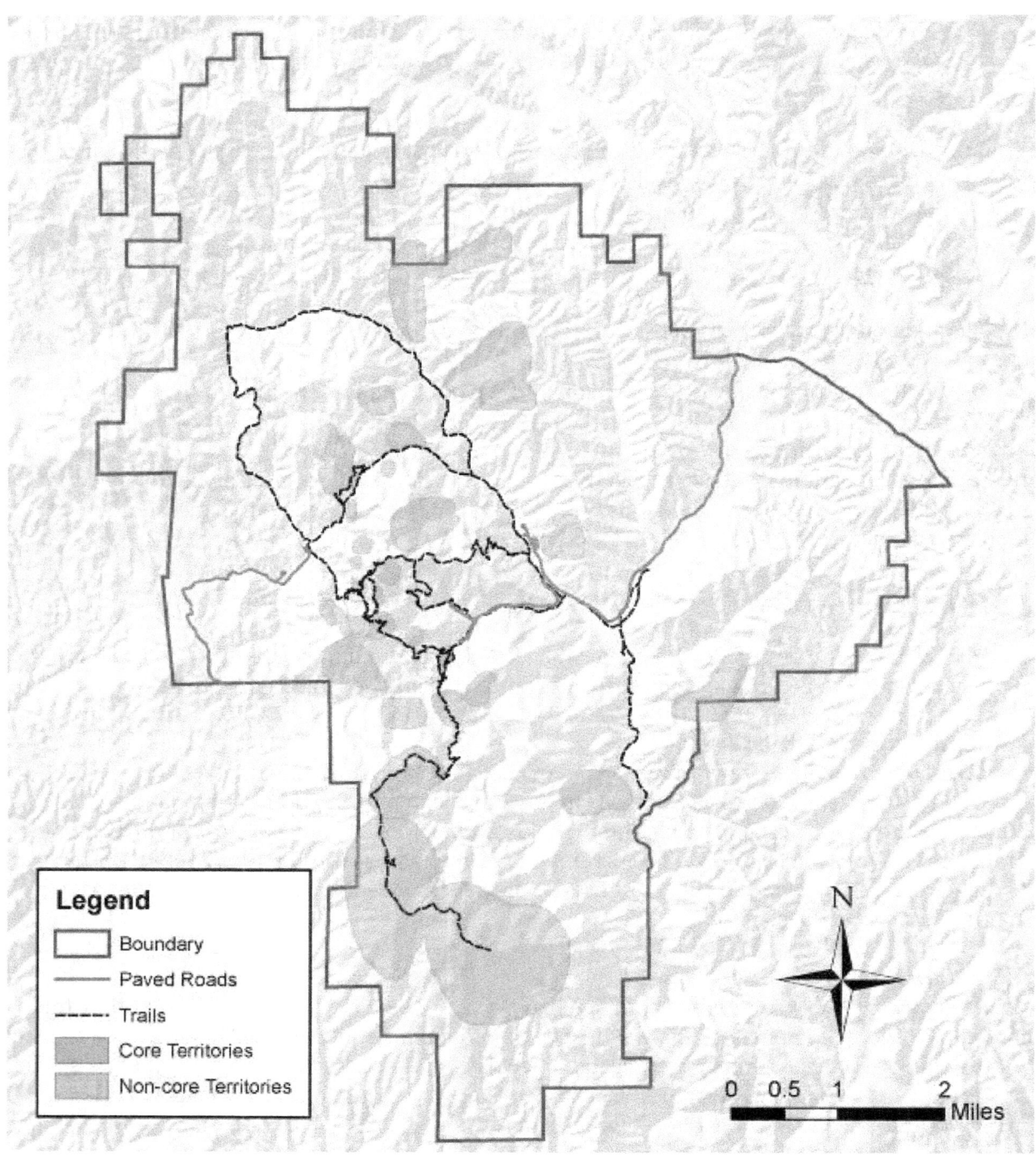

Figure 1. Historical territories near climbing routes (core) and throughout the rest of the park (non-core).

Of the raptor species that occur at PINN, the species that are at greatest risk of being impacted by human presence and disturbance in riparian habitats include: Cooper's hawks (*Accipiter cooperii*), sharp-shinned hawks, white-tailed kites (*Elanus leucurus*), and long-eared owls. While the lack of consistent nesting data for these species over the course of the 20-year raptor monitoring program precludes trend analysis on these species, the data provide park managers valuable information on the locations of important breeding areas. This information has been used for planning purposes relating to the revision of the PINN General Management Plan, guided timing of routine maintenance activities, as well as improved understanding of the diversity of breeding raptors at PINN.

1.6 Trigger for Management Activities

In addition to establishing and maintaining climbing advisories, raptor monitoring directly supports management activities. In past years, for example, data collection activities helped document illegal activities such as base jumping that caused disturbances to nesting falcons. In this example, the documentation informed law enforcement rangers and led to convictions of jumpers in a federal court (Emmons 2006).

Over the long-term, the power analysis presented below, indicates that monitoring will allows us to determine a 50% decline in territorial occupancy, hatching, or fledgling rates over 10 years with relatively high precision. Because waiting for 10 years is not ideal, park managers have set intermediate assessment points that will serve as early warnings to avert an unrecoverable crisis (see Bennetts et al. 2007). The assessment points will trigger a review of the data to evaluate if a decline is likely to be occurring, if obvious causes of a decline can be discerned, and if management actions should be considered. The first assessment points is met after noting a 25% decline of territory occupancy, hatching, or fledgling rates after 5 years of monitoring. A second assessment point is met after a 35% decline occurs in 7 years.

If declines are noted and they are likely due to disturbances from park visitors, management options may include (but are not limited to) additional visitor education, increased staffing to better monitor climbing and hiking activities in critical areas, or increased limitations to climbing and off-trail hiking during the raptor breeding season. If causes for declines are poorly understood, additional research may be triggered. The assessment points will help the park identify funding sources and implement research before a 50% decline over 10 years is realized. Research would be designed to discern cause and effect to identify appropriate management response. Food availability, for example, may play a significant role in understanding prairie falcon occupancy and reproductive success but at present, it is poorly understood (Buranek 2006).

2 - Sampling Design

Raptors are notoriously difficult to monitor (Marzluff et al. 1994; Dunk 1995; McFadzen and Marzluff 1996; Marzluff et al. 1997; Steenhof 1998; Bildstein and Meyer 2000; Kochert et al. 2002). Raptors are secretive and occur in low densities, making them difficult to monitor using typical methods like Variable Circle Plot Point Counts (Ralph et al. 1993). In general, the accepted methodology involves identifying suitable nesting areas and locating and observing nests (Steenhof 1987), with a minimum of two to three nest observation visits per breeding season (Fuller and Mosher 1981; Fraser et al. 1983; Steenhof 1987). With such a low sampling frequency, it is virtually impossible to attain reliable productivity information and essentially only allows for determining presence/absence of breeding pairs in a given area. For determining absence of prairie falcon occupancy within a given territory, two to three visits, scheduled to occur in different sequential months, were considered adequate.

At PINN, however, raptor breeding activity and productivity is used to establish and evaluate climbing/hiking advisories every year (see Background and Objectives above). To meet this need, more frequent sampling is required. Frequent nest site observations also allow for more accurate estimates of feeding and copulation rates, and precise productivity and fledging dates. This section provides a general outline of the sampling strategy employed.

2.1 Population Being Monitored

Based on 20 years of monitoring, 36 potential prairie falcon territories have been identified at PINN. Of the 36 territories in the target population, 18 of these territories fall into the "core" area. The core area consists of territories that are more accessible to climbers and hikers. These areas have been surveyed more consistently and frequently over the last 22 years so that hiking/climbing pressure can be monitored during the breeding season. Another 18 non-core areas were identified and added to the sample over time. Due to the added monitoring importance of the core areas, the core and non-core areas will be treated as separate strata with core territories censused annually.

2.1.1 Territories

A falcon *territory* is defined as an area that contains, or has historically contained, at least one nest with a mated falcon pair. Within a territory, no more than one pair of a given species is known to have bred at one time. Falcons will defend their territory against the presence of conspecific individuals. Note that this definition is not synonymous with a nest site which is the specific location of a falcon nest, either current or historical. Each territory may contain multiple potential nest sites, but no more than one will be occupied each year. Surveying a territory entails watching for falcon activity in the area, and visually checking all known nest sites in the territory for occupancy. To ensure that all likely territories have been identified for monitoring, GIS was used to identify potential nest sites based on exposed substrates and slope (> 40 degrees; Figure 2). The resulting map demonstrated that all potential nest sites had been previously searched and could be discounted as likely nest sites. In most cases, the potential nest site habitat identified in the map, does not provide suitable ledges for nesting. Periodic searches of some potential nest site habitat areas, however, may be warranted to determine if the population is expanding into unlikely or unexpected habitats. See Glossary for more detailed definitions of nest site and territories.

All potential cliff-nest territories within the core area have been surveyed every year since 1987. All historical territories in core areas and a subset of territories in the non-core areas will be made annually.

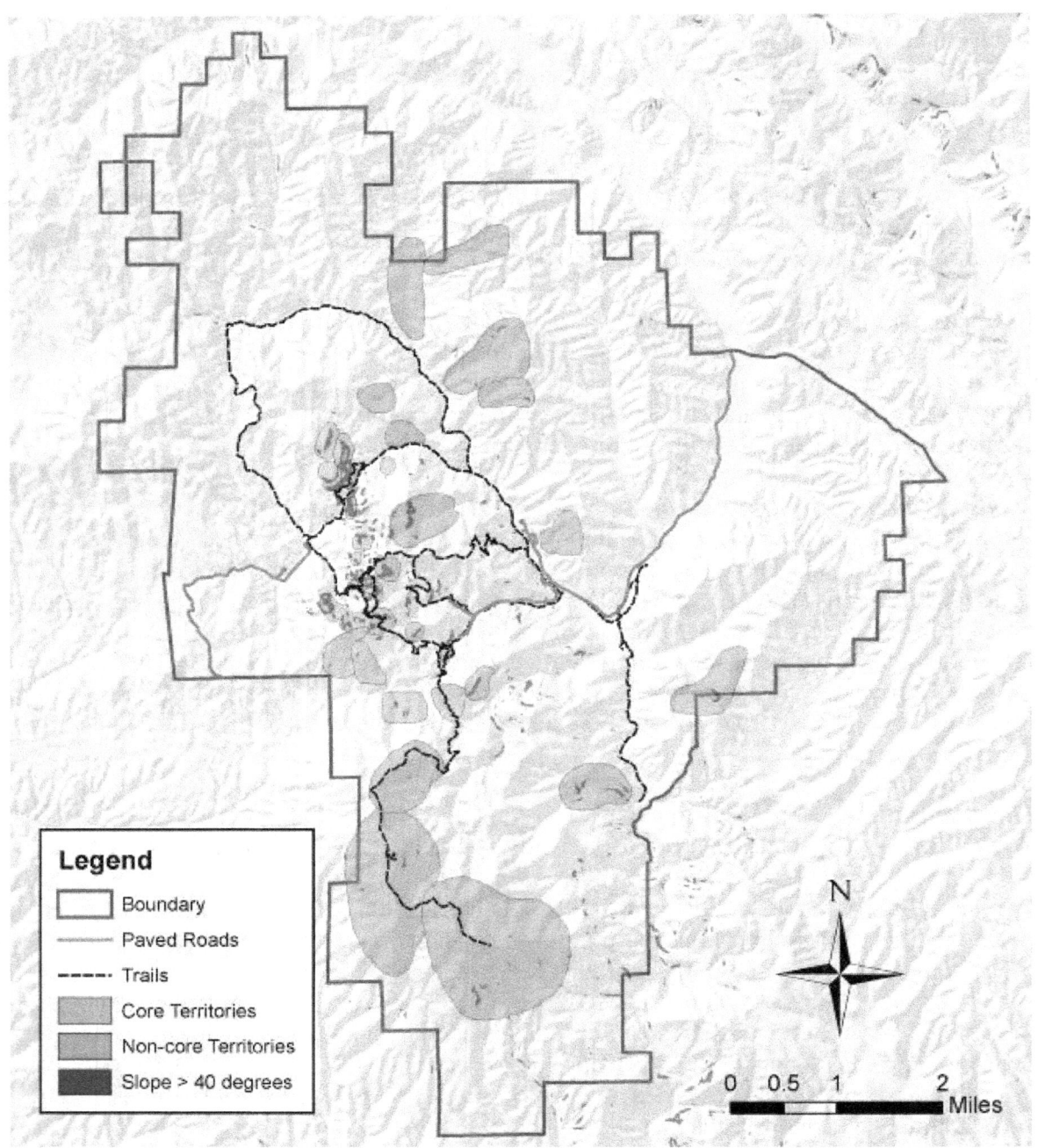

Figure 2. GIS map depicting potential nesting areas at PINN with >40 degree slopes. Field surveys, however, found that areas outside of core and non-core areas did not provide suitable nesting ledges.

2.2 Sampling Frequency and Replication

Occupancy and fecundity by territorial or nesting raptor pairs will be determined through an annual census of all core area territories and a sample of non-core areas. Sites are visited at least 3 times each year, spaced 21-28 days apart, with visits lasting 1 to 4 hours.

2.3.1 Sampling Frequency

Sampling will be limited to the raptor-breeding season (January through July). Site visits begin in January and the fledglings leave the nest by July.

Occupancy: To determine occupancy (presence of at least one prairie falcon), a maximum of three site visits will be made to historical nesting areas. Presence of a territorial prairie falcon on any of the three surveys confirms occupancy, and lack of presence after three surveys confirms lack of occupancy. In sites where prairie falcon detections are made, territorial occupancy is assessed by examining the behavior of each detected prairie falcon. Territorial behavior is verified by observing courtship or reproductive behavior or evidence of offspring.

Fecundity: To determine fecundity, nests are visited frequently enough to positively identify nesting stage including territorial occupancy, courtship, incubation, rearing of nestlings, and fledging of young within a breeding season (Fuller and Mosher 1981; Fraser et al. 1983; Steenhof 1987).

2.3.2 Intensified Sampling

Additional site visits are made to the territories in the core area (at least one visit every 7–14 days) to support establishment of advisory areas that protect breeding raptors from impacts of climbers and off-trail hikers at the park. To remain consistent, however, additional data on occupancy collected during these site visits are not included in comparisons made against non-core areas. These surveys are used only to inform management activities and interpret potential sources of nest failures/chick mortality during the nesting season.

2.3.3 Length of Site Visit

Three- to five-hour observation periods are commonly recommended to document territory occupancy of peregrine falcons and prairie falcons (U. S. Fish and Wildlife Service 1984; Cade et al. 1996; Smith and Hutchins 2006). Steenhof et al. (1999) employed 2-hour observation periods during point surveys to document territory occupancy of prairie falcons in the Snake River region of Idaho. To confirm absence of occupancy at potential falcon territories, we adopted a conservative standard of observing for at least 4 hours per visit. Site visits may be short (e.g., 1 hour) when breeding status can be quickly determined (e.g., when all nestlings at a nest site were clearly visible and easily aged) or they need to continue until at least 4 hours pass if territorial behaviors are not determined.

2.3 Sample Size and Statistical Power

The magnitude of levels of detectable trends in occupancy and fecundity metrics that are detectable are inextricably linked with the sample size precision of the estimator, the Type I error rate, and the statistical power considerations of the test used to assess the trend (Cohen 1988).

The Type I error rate, designated as α, is the probability of rejecting a true null hypothesis. For two-sided tests of trend, a Type I error would mean that the population was found to be changing when it was not. A Type II error occurs by failing to reject a false null hypothesis and thus concluding no change has occurred. For long-term monitoring, the cost of a Type I error may be far less than the cost of a Type II error. Mistakenly rejecting a true null hypothesis (Type I error) may trigger a management conservation action that is not actually needed. However, failing to detect a significant trend may have deleterious effects that cannot be reversed by the time the trend is actually detected. A conservative approach is to use a larger α value for higher power and reduced probability of a Type II error (Buhl-Mortensen 1996; Gibbs, et al. 1998; Mapstone 1995). For this power analysis, an α value of 0.20 is used. Power does not fall below the α value assumed for the trend test.

Starcevich and Steinhorst (2010; Appendix A) analyzed data collected from 2008 to 2009 to evaluate occupancy sampling design to reflect the current conditions the power to detect trends of prairie falcon occupancy. Pilot data collected prior to 2008 excluded some territories for which no detection was made, so these data were not used for the power analysis. This issue did not affect the fecundity data, so a separate analysis was conducted on data collected from 2002-2009 to evaluate fecundity sampling design. While fecundity data are available since 1984, the data collected since 2002 represent the current methodology and are thought to be more consistent.

2.3.1 Occupancy Analysis

Let y_{ijk} be the outcome for site i, year j, and visit k, and let y_{ijk} take a value of 1 if a prairie falcon is detected and 0 otherwise. Let y_{ijk} be the number of detections made at site i and year j during the kth visit. The zero-inflated binomial distribution is expressed as:

$$P\left(Y = y_{ijk}\right) = \pi_{ij} p_{ij}^{y_{ijk}} \left(1 - p_{ij}\right)^{1 - y_{ijk}} + \left(1 - \pi_{ij}\right) I\left(y_{ijk} = 0\right),$$

where π_j is the occupancy rate in year j and p_{ij} is the detection rate for site i and year j. Assume that there are S sites, T years, and K visits to a site each year. Define the indicator function as $I\left(y_{ij} = 0\right)$ as 1 when $y_{ij} = 0$ and 0 otherwise. This model assumes an equal number of visits to a site within a year, but K can vary among sites or among years.

Occupancy (π) is modeled with logistic regression as a function of related covariates:

$$\log\left(\frac{\pi_{ij}}{1 - \pi_{ij}}\right) = \gamma_0 + \gamma_1 x_{ij},$$

where x_{ij} represents a covariate for the ith site and the jth year. Multiple site-level or year-level covariates may be incorporated. To test for linear trend in the logged odds ratio of occupancy, the year covariate should be included as a predictor in the occupancy model. The probability of zero inflation (p) is simultaneously estimated by logistic regression:

$$\log\left(\frac{p_{ij}}{1-p_{ij}}\right) = \beta_0 + \beta'_1 x_{ijk},$$

where x_{ijk} represents a covariate collected at the ith site and k^{th} visit during the jth year.

The implicit dynamics occupancy model is assumed for this analysis. In contrast to the explicit dynamics model, estimates of colonization and local extinction are not explicitly measured in the implicit dynamics model (MacKenzie et al. 2006). The net effect of extinction and colonization rates on occupancy is monitored rather than estimating the parameters separately since monitoring net change over time is the primary goal.

Maximum likelihood is used to estimate the regression coefficients from the models for occupancy and detection rates. Occupancy can be modeled at the site-by-year level so predictors should be collected at the site level, year level, or site-by-year level. Detection probabilities are allowed to vary at each visit for each site and year, so covariates are often environmental covariates that vary from visit to visit (MacKenzie et al. 2006). However, if detection rates are also changing over time, a model that includes a year covariate may be needed for accurate occupancy estimation. Model selection is conducted using the Akaike Information Criterion (AIC). Model output is examined to be certain that valid variance estimates are obtained. When valid estimates of the variance cannot be acquired for the model with the lowest AIC, then the model with the lowest AIC and valid variance is used.

A prairie falcon detection does not necessarily imply that occupancy has been established. Designation of site occupancy requires multiple site visits within a year and evidence of territorial behavior. The power to detect a 50% decline in occupancy after 10 consecutive survey years is provided in Table 1. Because the core sites must be censused each year to monitor high-use areas, the power to detect trends in non-core sites was examined separately (Table 2). Comparisons of Tables 1 and 2 indicate that the high power to detect trends across the set of territories is largely due to the census of core sites. If occupancy is substantially different between the two subpopulations, then inference on prairie falcon occupancy at PINN may be misleading unless at least between 9 and 12 non-core territories are surveyed each year. However, the two years of pilot data did not indicate a significant difference in occupancy between core and non-core sites (p=0.1413).

Tables 1 and 2 also present revisit designs that specify the schedule of sites visitations by year for the duration of the monitoring period. Notations presented by MacDonald (2003) employ a string of numbers, dashes, and commas to identify the revisit design among panels. The numbers in odd-numbered positions will designate the number of consecutive visits to a panel before it rotates out of the revisit schedule. Digits in the even-numbered positions indicate the number of sampling occasions that the panel will not be revisited. Therefore, a revisit schedule of [1-0] indicates that the panel will be revisited each year and never rotated out of the schedule. This revisit schedule is equivalent to taking a random sample of sites and visiting them every year. The [1-n] revisit design represents a sampling design in which independent random samples are taken every year. A [2-2] revisit design consists of one panel visited for two consecutive years and then rested for two consecutive years before beginning the cycle again. Differing revisit

11

schedules among panels are indicated by separating the digits in parentheses by commas within the brackets. For example, a revisit schedule of [(1-0), (1-3)] indicates that the revisit design includes an annual panel that is revisited every year and four panels that are visited for one year then not visited for the following three years before being rotated back into the design. The [1-0] revisit design is known to have the highest power to detect trend (Urquhart and Kincaid 1999).

Table 1. Power to detect trend for different sample sizes and revisit designs.

Annual sample size of territories	Number of core sites surveyed annually	Number of non-core sites surveyed annually	Revisit design*	Power to detect a 50% decrease after 10 consecutive survey years
18	18	0	[1-0]	0.953
21	18	3	[1-0]	0.973
24	18	6	[(1-0),(1-4)]	1.000
30	18	12	[(1-0),(1-1)]	1.000
36	18	18	[1-0]	1.000

Table 2. Power to detect trend for non-core sites only.

Number of non-core sites surveyed annually	Revisit design	Power to detect a 50% decrease after 10 consecutive survey years
3	[1-0]	0.559
6	[1-0]	0.754
9	[1-0]	0.773
12	[1-0]	0.852

2.3.2 Fecundity Sample Design

Fecundity is monitored with counts of hatchlings or fledglings observed at each nest. These outcomes are also modeled with the zero-inflated binomial model. Let y_{ij} be the number of hatchlings or fledglings detected in occupied site i and year j. Let n be the number of occupied sites and T be the number of years monitored for fecundity. The probability mass function of Y is:

$$P\left(Y = y_{ij}\right) = \pi_{ij}\binom{M}{y_{ij}}p_{ij}^{y_{ij}}\left(1 - p_{ij}\right)^{M-y_{ij}} + \left(1 - \pi_{ij}\right)I\left(y_{ij} = 0\right),$$

where π_{ij} is the probability that an extra 0 is **not** observed at site i in year j, p_{ij} is the probability of a hatchling/fledgling at site i in year j, M is the maximum number of hatchlings/fledglings seen in any nest, and $I(y_{ij} = 0)$ is 1 when $y_{ij} = 0$ and is 0 otherwise. Maximum likelihood estimation is used to obtain estimates of the regression coefficients in each model, and the invariance property of maximum likelihood estimates is used to obtain estimates of π_{ij} and p_{ij}.

To test for trend in fecundity, the year covariate is included as a predictor in the binomial probability model and then tested for significance with a likelihood ratio test. In contrast to the occupancy analysis, fecundity inference is made on the change in p_{ij} over time.

Fecundity will be monitored by examining trends in the binomial probability of hatchlings and fledglings. The results of the power analysis indicate that annual surveys of at least 10 pair-occupied sites provides power of at least 0.8 to detect a 50% decline over 10 years in hatchling or fledgling rates (Tables 3 and 4; Starcevich and Steinhorst 2010).

Table 3. Power to detect a 50% decline in the number of hatchlings.

Annual sample size of occupied nests	Power to detect a 50% decrease after 10 years (based on 2002-2009 pilot data)
5	0.609
10	0.910
15	1.000
20	1.000
25	1.000

Table 4. Power to detect a 50% decline in the number of known fledglings.

Annual sample size of occupied nests	Power to detect a 50% decrease after 10 years (based on 2002-2009 pilot data)
5	0.645
10	0.922
15	0.977
20	1.000
25	1.000

Core sites are visited annually so that hiking and climbing pressure can be assessed throughout the breeding season. Given that the set of core sites is censused annually, power is examined for samples that contain all core sites and a range of non-core sites each year. For counts of both hatchlings (Table 5) and fledglings (Table 6), the power to detect trend in the binomial probability for each outcome is one. This level of power is attained even when no non-core sites are surveyed. However, if inference to non-core sites is of interest, then this subpopulation should be sampled with sufficient effort. Power to detect a 50% decline over 10 consecutive years exceeds 0.8 for as few as three sites each year for hatchlings (Table 7) and fledglings (Table 8).

Table 5. Power to detect trend in the binomial probability for **hatchlings** for a census of core sites and a sample of non-core sites.

Annual sample size of territories	Number of core sites surveyed annually	Number of non-core sites surveyed annually	Power to detect a 50% decrease after 10 consecutive survey years
18	18	0	1.000
21	18	3	1.000
24	18	6	1.000
30	18	12	1.000
36	18	18	1.000

Table 6. Power to detect trend in the binomial probability for **fledglings** for a census of core sites and a sample of non-core sites.

Annual sample size of territories	Number of core sites surveyed annually	Number of non-core sites surveyed annually	Power to detect a 50% decrease after 10 consecutive survey years
18	18	0	1.000
21	18	3	1.000
24	18	6	1.000
30	18	12	1.000
36	18	18	1.000

Table 7. Power to detect trend in the binomial probability for **hatchlings** for non-core sites only.

Number of non-core sites surveyed annually	Revisit design	Power to detect a 50% decrease after 10 consecutive survey years
3	[1-0]	0.875
6	[1-0]	0.957
9	[1-0]	1.000
12	[1-0]	1.000

Table 8. Power to detect trend in the binomial probability for **fledglings** for non-core sites only.

Number of non-core sites surveyed annually	Revisit design	Power to detect a 50% decrease after 10 consecutive survey years
3	[1-0]	0.816
6	[1-0]	0.969
9	[1-0]	0.988
12	[1-0]	0.996

2.4 Sample Design Summary

The power analysis indicates that a census of the 18 core sites should provide power greater than 0.80 for trend detection. Because inference to the subpopulation of non-core sites is of interest, then at least 12 of the non-core sites will be surveyed each year for occupancy and 10 for fecundity (Table 9). To select the 12 non-core territories, we will randomly order the non-core sites and use that random order to allot territories to the panels. Stratified random sampling within the non-core subpopulation will allow inference to that subpopulation of territories. MacKenzie et al. (2006) recommend the [1-0] revisit design so that the additional unexplained variation due to rotating different territories into the survey in different years will not affect variance estimates and therefore the power to detect trends.

Table 9. Sample design *[(1-0),(1-2)]* for Pinnacles National Monument.

Panel	Core/ non-core	Year 1	2	3	4	5	6
1	Core	18	18	18	18	18	18
2	Non-core	6	6	6	6	6	6
3	Non-core	6			6		
4	Non-core		6			6	
5	Non-core			6			6
ANNUAL TOTAL		30	30	30	30	30	30

* At least 10 territories will be randomly drawn from each year's occupied territories to track fecundity (hatching and fledgling success).

3 - Field Methods

The Prairie falcon breeding season runs from late January until July. During that time, surveys are made of historical territories to determine if territories are occupied by single or paired birds. Once nests are located, repeated surveys are made to document any hatching and fledgling activities. To reduce disturbance to nesting falcons, the park establishes advisories around historical territories in the core areas at the beginning of the field season. Advisories are lifted around territories that are not occupied by the middle of the breeding season. All advisories are lifted by the end of the season.

3.1 Field Season Preparations

The field season begins with hiring a Raptor Technician by January of each year. For the first month, the technician becomes familiar with the protocol, SOPs, the project database, equipment, and data sheets. Training in field methods, including field note taking and locating territories, will be provided by the Wildlife Biologist at PINN. If data management training is needed, this will be provided by the SFAN Data Manager. If first-aid or other safety training is necessary, this will be provided by the park.

At the beginning of the field season, the technician gathers, checks, and becomes familiar with all of the required field equipment including binoculars, telescope, camera, data sheets, rangefinder, GPS, and the Kestrel weather meter with thermometer. Faulty equipment is repaired or replaced. A complete list of equipment is provided in SOP 1: Field Methods.

Climbing/hiking advisories are established around all core area territories occupied by prairie falcon, peregrine falcon, and golden eagle pairs within any of the last 3 years. While advisories are not closures, any visitors found within advisory areas can be cited and fined by park law enforcement staff. Advisories are established by posting signs at trailheads, posting updates to bulletin boards, notifying appropriate staff, "Friends Groups", and sending press releases to various media outlets. Locations for posting signs are presented in SOP 1: Field Methods.

3.2 Field Season Surveys

Surveys begin by late January or early February when prairie falcons begin establishing territories. All historical territories in the core areas and 12 selected territories in the non-core areas are selected for monitoring occupancy and fecundity annually. Although only 12 non-core territories are selected for monitoring to determine both occupancy and fecundity trends, the park has consistently contributed funding to supplement the monitoring budget over the last seven years so that all non-core territories can be tracked each year to meet management requirements.

Territories are observed from watch spots. Directions and maps are provided in SOP 2: Watch Spot Locations. It will be helpful for the technician to plan survey routes to maximize the number of territories visited without retracing steps. For example, when visiting North Balconies, raptor activity may also be seen en route at Guard Rock (at the foot of Pig Canyon), along Old Pinnacles Trail, at the North Wilderness Trail junction, and at Eagle Rock. While observing North Balconies, raptor activity may also be seen at Crowley, Machete, the Balconies Cave Trail junction, etc. Routing suggestions are provided in both SOP 1: Field Methods and SOP 2: Watch Spot Locations.

Unpredictable weather (e.g., rain, fog) necessitates maintaining some flexibility in scheduling site visits throughout the season. While light rain or mist would not cancel surveys, moderate or heavy rain will terminate surveys if visibility is impaired or if trails become too slippery and unsafe. Lightning always results in a cancellation of surveys for safety considerations.

Initially, most fieldwork is conducted from mid-afternoon to evening when territorial raptors at PINN are most active in the park and visible. During daytime, falcons are typically outside of the park to feed. The birds typically return to the breeding areas in the park toward dusk. Most observations will take place just before raptors fly into cliff crevices to roost for the night.

Each territory will be visited at <u>least</u> three times to determine occupancy, with each visit in a different month. The technician spends up to four hours observing at each site before concluding that a territory is unoccupied. Observations are typically made through binoculars or telescope depending on distance from watch spot to the territory. Data are collected on a standard datasheets each time that a territory is visited. The same territory may be seen from multiple watch spots. Additional data may be collected following the Grinnellian method in a running diary style for birds sighted and associated behaviors observed. Data noted on the datasheet includes name of the territory, date, weather conditions (including air speed and thermometer collected with a weather meter), number of birds sighted, territorial behavior (e.g., territorial displays, food exchanges between males and females, copulations, food exchanges between males and females, use of perches or night roosts), and nesting behavior (e.g., incubation, food carries, nest switches). The datasheet also includes space to draw maps of nest or perching locations. If territorial behaviors that define occupancy are observed in less than four hours, the technician may move on to a watch spot in another territory.

As soon as all prairie falcon pairs have chosen nest sites, usually in late March to mid-April, advisories are lifted for unoccupied territories. Staff is notified, bulletin boards are updated, and notifications are sent out to climbing shops. During the nesting period, prairie falcons may be found during any time of the day. The number of eggs in a nest should be documented if visible from the watch spot. Observations of nests are made frequently enough to document the number and timing of hatching. The length of observations will depend largely on how cooperative the birds are to allow the documentation of eggs or hatchlings.

After raptors hatch, the technician estimates ages of young on <u>at least</u> 3 monitoring visits to accurately estimate fledging dates. Two weeks after fledging has finished, usually in June or July, climbing / hiking advisories at the park are lifted.

On a daily basis data sheets and notebooks need to be reviewed for completeness. Throughout the field season, data are transcribed from data sheets and notebook into the database (described below and SOP 3: Data Management). Data are verified by the data manager at the end of the season.

3.3 Ancillary Data
In addition to tracking prairie falcons, collection of presence/absence and productivity information of all other breeding raptor species at PINN is important to park managers. The

technician will conduct surveys in non cliff habitats to determine species diversity, nesting, productivity, and phenology of other raptors in the park as time allows. Most of these surveys are made on the way to and from watch spots. It is recognized that because these data are not collected with systematic, standardized sample efforts, population trends cannot be determined with statistical estimates of certainty.

Given the recent breeding records of peregrine falcons at PINN in 2005–2007 and the similarity of nesting habits between peregrine and prairie falcons (Hickey 1942, 1969; Bond 1946; Olsen and Olsen 1978, 1980; Porter et al. 1987; Cade et al. 1996; Steenhof 1998; White et al. 2002), breeding peregrine falcons will be documented and monitored according to the measurable objectives and sampling designs outlined for prairie falcons. As the amount of data for peregrine falcons mounts, it may be possible to conduct statistical trend analyses in the future.

Beginning in December 2003, PINN and the Ventana Wildlife Society (VWS) began a California Condor Recovery Program at PINN. Breeding pairs of California condors were thought to occur at PINN through the 1930's, and solitary birds were seen into the 1980's. After years of releases, the first condors have nested in PINN in 2010. The PINN condors are closely monitored and actively managed by the PINN and VWS biologists. Once a population is reestablished, a formal long-term monitoring program will be developed.

3.4 End of the Field Season
At the end of the field season, all remaining advisories are taken down. Staff, "Friends Groups", and media are informed of the lifted advisories. Equipment including scope, tripod, binoculars, rangefinders, etc. is cleaned and stored at the Resource Management Office. Any remaining data are entered, verified, and archived as described below. An annual report is written and circulated as described below and in SOP 5: Data Analysis and Reporting. Photos and project highlights are submitted to the network program manager for the network's annual report. End of season procedures are further detailed in SOP 1: Field Methods.

4 - Data Management

4.1 Management of Statistical Data

All data used to meet the monitoring objectives are maintained in the Raptor Monitoring Database (S:\RRM\RRM_Data\RM Workgroups\PROJECTS\Breeding Raptors\database\important database files). The database, includes data for prairie falcon productivity for each year (from 1987 onward), including nesting pairs, successful nests, young of year (YOY) hatched, YOY fledged, and fledglings/nest throughout the park (core and non-core areas together), and specifically in core areas. These data are listed in SOP 5: Data Analysis and Reporting. The numeric data are the culmination of field monitoring observations and data entry into the PINN raptor monitoring databases described below. The numeric data stored in this database are used by biometricians working with park staff to determine prairie falcon productivity and population trends over 3-5-year intervals, as described further in the Data Summaries and Analysis section below.

4.2 Overview of Database Design

The San Francisco Bay Area Network Inventory and Monitoring Program (SFAN) staff has developed a relational Microsoft (MS) Access XP database for the raptor monitoring program at PINN compliant with the Natural Resource Database Template (NRDT) Version 3.1, an application developed by the NPS Natural Resource Inventory and Monitoring Program (I&M). The data are organized around survey events from fixed observation points, which are described and geographically defined in a locations table. Besides actual raptor observations, copulation, and feeding events, the database is used to maintain records of end-of-season summaries of occupancy and breeding phenology, data history, field personnel, photo records, and media contact addresses. The raptor database has a separate front-end (user interface) and back-end (data tables). The user interface for the database is modeled after the NRDT Front-end Application Builder (FAB) Version 1.0, an MS Access user-interface template designed by the NPS Natural Resource GIS Program. The database is further described in SOP 3: Data Management.

4.3 Data Entry and Verification

Data entry is best performed by a person who is familiar with the data and ideally takes place as soon as data collection is complete. The single goal of data entry is the transcription of the data from paper records into the computer with 100% accuracy. However, because transcription errors are virtually unavoidable during data entry, they will have to be corrected during the data verification process. Observation of certain data entry guidelines, however, will minimize verification work. The SFAN Data Manager, in conjunction with the PINN Wildlife Biologist, should provide training in the use of the database to all data entry technicians and any other users. The Wildlife Biologist will ensure that data entry technicians understand how to enter data and that they follow the protocol. Specific procedures for entering data into the project database are detailed in SOP 3: Data Management.

The most robust quality assurance and quality control (QA/QC) measures for data entry are built into the raptor database design. Several additional QA/QC procedures must be followed by the database user:

- Have a familiarity with the database software, database structure, and any standard codes for data entry that have been developed.
- Enter data in a timely manner. All data should be entered into the project database as soon as possible, preferably no less than once a week.
- Enter the data, one logical "set" at a time. Record in a notebook any known errors or any questions that arise about the data content; these will be useful during data verification. Initial and date each paper form as it is completed to avoid confusion about what has been entered and what has not with a different color then the data.
- Interrupt data entry only at logical stopping points. When reaching stopping points, make a working backup copy of the data for safety's sake if the software does not do so automatically.

Manual effort is generally required to get data into electronic format. Any typographical errors made will accumulate in the permanent database unless the data are verified and the errors detected. By implementing data verification procedures, these errors can be reduced, if not eliminated. Data verification immediately follows data entry and involves checking the accuracy of computerized records against the original source, usually hard copy field records, and identifying and correcting any errors. When the computerized data are verified as accurately reflecting the original field data, the paper forms can be archived and most data manipulation can be done on the computer.

The prairie falcon monitoring program utilizes visual and audio review after data entry for data verification. Visual review after data entry requires two people. One person sits with the field datasheets in hand while the other sits at the computer with the database open. As data sheets are read aloud, the database record is followed and analyzed for data entry errors. Errors are corrected as they are discovered. Verified data sheets should be dated and initialed.

4.4 Metadata and Data Archival Procedures

The NPS GIS Committee recently required all NPS GIS data layers be described with the NPS Metadata Profile, which combines the Federal Geographic Data Committee (FGDC) standard, elements of the ESRI metadata profile, the Biological Data Profile, and NPS-specific elements. Although no standard has been applied to natural resource databases, the SFAN will complete the NPS Metadata Profile to the greatest extent possible to document databases developed for the SFAN I&M program.

A complete metadata record for the raptor monitoring MS Access database will be generated in compliance with current NPS standards by the SFAN data manager. When completed, the metadata record, but not the data themselves, will be posted to the NPS Data Store for public discovery and consumption. Contact information within the metadata record will direct interested parties to the Network Data Manager for further inquiries. The metadata record posted to the NPS Data Store will be updated annually after the annual data has been entered and error-checked or following database revision to a new version whole number (i.e., v1_3 to v2_0, but not v2_0 to v2_1).

Each season, once data entries have been entered and proofed, the physical documents, including datasheets, field notebooks, printouts of end-of-season reports, nest data forms for CDFG and

SCPBRG, are all kept in the Research and Resource Management (RRM) office, in a fire-proof cabinet in folders, each marked by subject and year. The archived photo negatives and photo prints are also kept in the RRM office in another fire-proof cabinet as detailed in the photo management section above.

All digital documents and data related to the raptor monitoring program, including scanned and digital photos, are stored on the "SharedData" drive on the PINN file server Inppinn001.

At the SFAN offices at Golden Gate National Recreation Area (GOGA), copies of all final documents and digital data relating to the raptor monitoring program are archived on the Marin Headlands server at:
Inpgogamahe1\Divisons\Network I&M\IM_Archive\VS_Indicators\Raptors

Data and documents are stored in separate folders. The raptor database will be copied and archived here annually after that year's field data has been entered and error-checked. All final documents relating to the raptor monitoring program, including the protocol and all annual reports, will also be stored in the raptor archive directory. All files in the archive directory are stored in read-only format.

5 - Analysis and Reporting

Reporting and analysis are essential components of the raptor monitoring process. The effectiveness of the PINN raptor monitoring study over the past 20 years lies not only in the field work and data management, but also in how the information gathered is shared throughout the season and how it is summarized at the end of the season. Reporting within-season allows for the information gathered to be transferred to Law Enforcement and Interpretation Rangers for the most effective internal support of the program. It also allows visitors to understand what Resource Management does in a NPS unit and how resources are protected while providing for visitor enjoyment of those resources. Data analysis at the end of the season allows for consistent scientific rigor to be applied to the raptor monitoring program, and allows resource managers to identify prairie falcon population and productivity trends and triggers for management actions and resource protections.

5.1 Reporting Schedule and Formats

Reporting results is a critical component of long-term vital signs monitoring in order to ensure that information generated through the program is available to all levels of park management including planning, interpretation, maintenance, and law enforcement. A summary of reports that will be developed is provided in Table 10 and details are provided in SOP 5: Data Analysis and Reporting.

5.1.1 Bi-Weekly Update

One of the most critical components of updating park staff about active nesting territories and climbing advisories is the Bi-Weekly Update. The Updates include the following information: the number of territorial and nesting raptor pairs, which territories are occupied and the status of each territory (e.g., defense, incubation, nestlings including number and age). Any unique or noteworthy observations (new territories or nests, unusual raptor sightings, etc.) are also included. The Updates are distributed to all employees via e-mail. Because updates are also distributed to organizations and individuals not associated with PINN, specific nest locations are **not** disclosed.

5.1.2 Annual Report

The post-season or annual report provides a concise summary of the field season, enables readers to determine if the goals of the project are being met and provides an administrative and scientific record of monitoring activities. Format follows the national guidelines established for Natural Resource Reports in the Natural Resource Publications Management guidance (NRPM; http://nature.nps.gov/publications/NRPM). The annual report content includes an abstract, introduction, study area and methods, results, discussion and conclusion. The results section of the report summarizes the following:

1. Effort: hours of observations made during the season.

2. Occupancy Status: identifies the total number of territories occupied by singles and pairs; lists occupancy status of each territory monitored.

3. Fecundity Status: identifies the total number of nests, number of successful nests (at least one egg hatched), and number of hatchlings and fledglings. The reproductive outcome of each nest monitored is provided along with causes of nest failure, if known.

4. Phenology: list dates of first arrivals, hatch dates, and fledging dates.

5. Human Interactions: indicates nesting activity that may have been affected by human interaction. Notes include which territories may have been affected and if any actions were taken by staff.

Table 10. Summary of reporting and communication products.

Communication Product	Schedule	Summary
Annual Report	Annually	• Archive data and document monitoring activities • Describe current condition of the resources • Document changes in the monitoring protocol
Analysis and Synthesis Report	3–5 years	• Determine patterns and trends • Discover correlations among resources being monitored • Analyze data to determine the level of change that can be detected using the existing sampling scheme • Provide context, interpret data for the park within a multi-park, regional, or national context • Recommend changes to management practices
Program and Protocol Reviews	5 years	• Periodic formal reviews of operations and results • Review of protocol design and product to determine if changes are needed • Part of the quality assurance – peer review process
Executive Briefing	Annually (upon completion of annual report)	• Two-page summary that lists monitoring objectives and questions, discusses annual results, and provides a regional context.
Bi-weekly Update	Bi-Weekly during the field season.	• Brief update listing species and names of active territories. Highlights areas where advisories are in effect.
Quarterly IM Update	Quarterly	• This one-page monthly e-mail provides park staff with a short update on vital signs projects. Text should be no more than one paragraph.

The discussion section of the annual report provides a context for each year's result in comparison to previous years. Recommendations including management, research, and changes in the protocol (changing monitoring intervals and timing, moving/adding sites, etc.) will also be included in the discussion.

These annual reports will be distributed to the SFAN parks, and can be used for park management reporting. Portions may be included in the network's Annual Administrative Report and Work Plan (AARWP).

5.1.3 Analysis and Synthesis Report

A comprehensive data analysis and synthesis will be written every 3–5 years to summarize general trends in prairie falcon occupancy and fecundity. Having more than three years of monitoring data are available, linear trends in the logged odds of occupancy and fecundity may be estimated and tested for significance. Having this extra time allows for more thorough data analysis and review of protocols and may give greater opportunity for adaptive management.

Format follows the national guidelines established for Natural Resource Reports in the Natural Resource Publications Management guidance (NRPM; http://nature.nps.gov/publications/NRPM). The report content includes an abstract, introduction, study area and methods, results, discussion and conclusion.

The main focus of this report will be to determine patterns and trends of prairie falcon population change and nesting success. This will allow the staff to assess whether the data from the last several years fall within the historical "natural range of variability".

The key analyses presented in the report will be:

Occupancy: Occupancy estimates will be obtained annually and will provide measures of status. When more than three years of monitoring data are available, linear trends in the logged odds of occupancy may be estimated and tested for significance. The number of detections is modeled as a zero-inflated binomial random variable (MacKenzie et al. 2006). To test for trend in occupancy, the year covariate is included as a predictor in the occupancy model and then tested for significance with a likelihood ratio test.

Fecundity: Fecundity estimates will be obtained annually and will provide measures of status. When more than three years of monitoring data are available, linear trends in the logged odds of the binomial probability of fecundity may be estimated and tested for significance. The number of detections is modeled as a zero-inflated binomial random variable (MacKenzie et al. 2006). To test for trend in fecundity, the year covariate is included as a predictor in the binomial probability model and then tested for significance with a likelihood ratio test.

Methodology for trend analysis of occupancy and fecundity rates is provided in SOP 5 Appendix A, and pilot data are provided in SOP 5 Appendix B. Instructions are given for the VGAM package of the R Project for Statistical Computing. The VGAM package is used for obtaining maximum likelihood estimates from zero-inflated mixture distributions.

In addition to reporting trends in occupancy and fecundity, the analysis and synthesis report will:

- Provide context and interpret data for the park within a multi-park, regional, or national context.
- Demonstrate if management triggers have been met.

- Discover correlations among resources being monitored.
- Recommend any changes to monitoring and/or management practices.
- List research questions.

6 - Operational Requirements

6.1 Roles and Responsibilities

The network Raptor Technician (GS-7) is responsible for conducting field work, data entry, and communicating results to some degree. The position is seasonal (Dec – July) and will have a flexible schedule ("maxi-flex") due to the need for travel time and long hours in the field. The duty station will be at the PINN headquarters. The park provides office space and administrative support. The technician is directly supervised by the PINN wildlife biologist (GS-9/11). The supervisor provides training and consistency in implementing the protocol.

The data management aspect of the monitoring effort is the shared responsibility of the program manager and raptor technician. Typically, the raptor technician is responsible for data collection, data entry, data verification and validation, as well as data summary, analysis and reporting. The wildlife biologist is ultimately responsible for adequate quality assurance/quality control (QA/QC) procedures built into the database management system and appropriate data handling procedures followed by raptor technician.

6.1.1 Tasks for the SFAN Raptor Technician:
- Be well-versed in all aspects of the SFAN prairie falcon monitoring protocol and conduct protocol revisions.
- Coordinate logistics for field work.
- Coordinate field assistance for protocol implementation and provide training to field assistants such as volunteers.
- Maintain equipment in good working order and keep maintenance records.
- Collect field data and implement field QA/QC measures.
- Coordinate data entry, verification, and validation and consult with network data managers.
- Perform basic statistical analyses on data; present and interpret results in annual reports.
- Coordinate with PINN Wildlife Biologist regarding staff and training needs, data analysis and data interpretation.
- Coordinate with PINN Wildlife Biologist regarding budget, vehicle, and equipment needs.
- Complete Bi-Weekly Updates, annual report and other communication products.

6.1.2 Broad Tasks for PINN Wildlife Biologist
- Provide technical assistance and supervision for the SFAN Raptor Technician.
- Develop and conduct performance review (to be reviewed by network coordinator).
- Manage prairie falcon monitoring program budget.
- Provide or coordinate training for the SFAN Raptor Technician.
- Conduct annual QA/QC field checks.
- Present issues with Network Ecologist for consultation with the Technical Advisory Committee.
- Reviews and provides comments on annual report.
- Initiates and completes analysis and synthesis report.

6.1.3 Tasks for Network Data Manager
- Provide assistance to the Network Raptor Technician regarding data management, archiving, reporting
- Assist with GIS needs
- Assist with compilation of metadata for past and current monitoring programs

6.1.4 Broad Tasks for Network Program Manager
- Coordinate guidance on data management, data analysis and reporting
- Provide information related to I&M program requirements including reporting requirements and deadlines
- Review technical reports and provide programmatic oversight
- Plan program budget in coordination with Wildlife Biologist
- Coordinate peer review of analysis and synthesis reports

Broad tasks for the SFAN I&M Network Program Manager are not included in the project budget below (Table 11).

6.2 Budget

Personnel expenses for field work are based on using one raptor technician (GS-07 Raptor Technician) for 15 pay periods. All of the territories are accessed via hiking either from the Eastside Headquarters or Chalone Maintenance Yards, thus minimal travel costs are expected. Equipment including binoculars, scope, tripod, GPS, digital camera are long-lasting but may need to be replaced from time to time.

Additional periodic costs may be incurred if new equipment (e.g., spotting scopes and binoculars) are needed beyond those allowable by the annual budget. Periodic costs may also include expense for technical assistance through cooperative agreements (e.g., through a NPS cooperative ecosystem studies unit) or contracts to assist with long-term data analysis if these needs can not be met by park or SFAN staff.

We estimate that approximately 30% of the budget is allocated to data management and reporting. Most of the data entry is done by the raptor technician throughout the field season. The final two pay periods is dedicated to data quality control, data analysis, report writing. The network's data manager also assists with data management and reporting throughout the season.

The majority of the long-term funding is provided through the SFAN I&M Program. Table 11 also indicates that Pinnacles provides significant funding. Funding from the park is allocated to allow the raptor technician to conduct a full census of prairie falcon territories in both the core and non-core areas and to track breeding activities of other raptor species in the park. While all of the raptor data are tracked through the program's database, long-term trends are only for prairie falcons. If budget shortfalls occur, the decision to monitor species other than prairie falcons may be revisited. Similarly, the desire to make inference to the non-core areas may be revisited and the number of territories monitored could be reduced.

Table 11. Annual budget for FY09.

Description	Category	Amount
Funding Source	Park Contribution (PINN)	$10,000
	SFAN I&M Contribution	$27,000
	Sub-Total	$37,000
Expense Type	Raptor Technician GS-7/4, 15 pp	$26,000
	Data Manager GS-11, 1–2 pp	$4,000
	Wildlife Biologist, PINN GS-11, 1–2 pp	$4,000
	Vehicle	$2,000
	Equipment and Supplies	$500
	Travel	$500
	Sub-Total	$37,000*
	Balance	$0

* Approximately 30% of budget is allocated to data management by raptor technician and data manager.

6.3 Qualifications and Training
The raptor technician must be able to visually and/or aurally identify birds, and be proficient at interpreting breeding behavior. Training requirements are discussed in SOP 1: Field Methods.

6.4 Annual Workload and Field Schedule
Raptor monitoring will begin in early January and will continue through fledging, usually from mid-June to mid-July (Table 12). The first month of fieldwork is dedicated to training and orientation. Monitoring efforts will require, at a minimum, 1 full time raptor technician who works 5 days a week. An additional person available 1–2 days per week would greatly enhance the data collected. Each territory should be visited once every 7–28 days. Only one territory can be visited in a day during territory establishment and in general for the entire season. On occasion two territories can be visited during incubation and nestling rearing – but only if travel time between the territories is short. Inclement weather (primarily rain or low fog) will preclude the scheduling of sampling events to specific annual dates. At the end of each field season, 1–2 payperiods are needed to write the annual report, complete data entry and perform data QA/QC, which should be completed by the end of July.

6.5 Facility and Equipment Needs
The nature of bird survey work does not require special facilities beyond normal office space and equipment storage needs. A table of field equipment needs for one raptor technician is listed in SOP 1: Field Methods. If two or more raptor technicians work simultaneously, equipment requirements will increase accordingly. Computer equipment for data entry and report writing will be supplied by PINN.

Table 12. Summary of annual work schedule (Jan–Aug).

	Jan	Feb	Mar	Apr	May	Jun	Jul	Aug
Prepare for field season	Organize equipment							
Field surveys	Training	Locate territories /nests	Locate territories /nests	Locate territories /nests/ young	Young/ fledglings	Fledglings	Survey end	
Maintain climbing/ hiking advisories	Establish advisories			Updated advisories		Lift advisories		
Press releases to media								
Bi-weekly highlights sent to park staff								
Write annual report								

6.6 Permit Procedures

All data collection consists of field observations collected along or near existing trails. The procedures are considered non-invasive and are no different that activities that might be conducted by any park visitor. Research permits are, therefore, not needed by the park.

6.7 Procedures for Revising the Protocol

Over time, revisions to both the Protocol Narrative and to specific SOPs are to be expected. Careful documentation of changes to the protocol, and a library of previous protocol versions are essential for maintaining consistency in data collection and for appropriate treatment of the data during data summary and analysis. The MS Word documents for each monitoring component contain a 'Revision History Log' that identifies which version of the protocol was being used when the data were collected. The steps for changing the protocol (either the Protocol Narrative or the SOPs) are outlined in SOP 4: Revising the Protocol. Each SOP contains a Revision History Log that should be filled out each time a SOP is revised to explain why the change was made, and to assign a new Version Number to the revised SOP. The new version of the SOP and/or Protocol Narrative should then be archived in the network protocol library under the appropriate folder (SFAN Network/ Individual Vital Signs). SOP 4 also includes peer review comments on previous version of the protocol along with the authors' responses to document rationale for changes to the document.

7 - Glossary

Adult: a raptor characterized by adult plumage and coloration.

Advisory: management action or technique used at PINN to protect cliff-nesting raptors from potential human disturbance, through enactment of voluntary climbing and off-trail hiking closures to all core areas in the park used by nesting raptors in a given season. Advisories are in effect each breeding season from early January until 2 weeks after the last fledging of cliff-nesting raptors in a core area affected by the advisories, usually by mid-July. Advisories are not closures because they are based on visitors voluntarily refraining from climbing and hiking off-trail in core areas affected by the advisories. Also called "climbing / hiking advisories" because the advisories directly impact these visitor activities.

Advisory areas: locations within core areas that are affected by advisories, as detailed in press releases, park bulletin boards, bi-weekly raptor updates distributed to park staff through email, and informational brochures distributed by the PINN interpretative division.

Apteria: bare featherless area between pterylae or feather tracts.

Auriculars: feathers covering the ear opening and the area immediately around it.

Base jumping: the activity or sport of parachuting from a high structure (as a building, tower, or bridge) or cliff.

Bill-swipe: a technique used by prairie and peregrine falcons in courtship and nest preparation, in which an adult falcon swipes and shovels at the soil of a prospective nest site to shape it for a scrape.

Breeding season: period from the start of nest-building (refurbishment) or courtship to independence of fledged young.

Brood size at fledging: the number of young produced by successful pairs.

Clutch size: the number of eggs laid in a nest.

Core area: encompasses historic prairie falcon territories where climbing impacts could occur based on the proximity to climbing routes. The territory names for these locations are as follows: Crowley Towers, South Balconies, North Balconies, Scout Peak, Goat Rock, Resurrection Wall, Tunnel, Teapot Dome, Egg, Hawkins Peak, Pipsqueak Pinnacles, Frog / Hand, Little Pinnacles. See also Figure 2.

Coronal region: the area on top of the head.

Coverts: small feathers that overlie or cover the bases of the large flight feathers of the wings and tail.

Eyass: a young or nestling raptor still in the nest and not yet fledged. Also spelled "eyas."

Eechip: a call made by prairie and peregrine falcons in courtship, greetings, nest switches, food exchanges, and occasionally during territorial defense. The term "eechip" is derived from the sound produced by the call.

Eyrie: the nest of a bird of prey. Also spelled "aerie."

Fecundity: used synonymously with productivity.

Fledged young: young raptors that have fledged or flown from the nest where they originally hatched. Can refer to raptor young that were not observed flying from a particular nest, but are recently fledged as evidenced by feather down still visible or confirmed food exchanges with adults. Interchangeable with "post-fledglings."

Fledging: a fully-feathered young raptor voluntarily leaving the nest for the first time.

Fledgling: young raptor that has just (within 1–5 days) fledged or become capable of flying from the nest where they hatched, confirmed through direct observation.

Hard incubation: an adult raptor or raptors consistently on eggs at a nest in incubation posture with periods of less than 20 consecutive minutes not on eggs. This can include nest switches involving both adults as long as the duration of the switch from one adult incubating eggs to another is less than 20 minutes.

Hatchling: a young raptor in the nest just hatched from an egg, 1–5 days old, not yet capable of thermoregulation.

Historical nest: see "nest site."

Immature: a fledged raptor – including juveniles, second-year birds, and sub-adults – that has not reached its adult form, maturity, or size, as distinguished by plumage, coloration, and body size.

Incubation period: the time between the start of incubation and the hatching of an egg, during which the egg is kept at or near body temperature by the parent.

Juvenal feathers: the sequence of flight feathers which replace the natal down.

Juvenile: a fledged raptor that still has not yet reached its second-year, sub-adult, or adult forms, maturity or size, as distinguished by plumage, coloration, and body size.

Natal down: first feathers to form on young birds, replaced by the development of juvenile feathers.

Nest: the structure made or the place used by birds for laying their eggs and sheltering their young.

Nest failure: Failure of a raptor nest to produce any fledglings, due to failure of eggs to hatch, or failure of nestlings to fledge. Egg failure can be due to abandonment by the adult nesting pair, eggs beings crushed in the nest, eggs falling out of nests, or eggs being predated. Nestling failure can be due to abandonment by the adult nesting pair, starvation, temperature extremes leading to death, nestlings falling out of the nest, or predation.

Nest selection: a site chosen by a raptor female and/or pair for nesting, as confirmed by observed incubation or nestling presence at the site. Prior to incubation, nest selection behavior includes regular visits to the site, clearing a scrape with feet or beak, adding nesting material to a site, laying down in and getting back up from the site, calling from the site with the mate following to perch at the site. However, these activities alone are not sufficient to determining nest selection; incubation and/or nestling presence at the site must be observed to confirm nest selection.

Nest site: a raptor nest, confirmed currently or historically by presence of raptor eggs or nestlings. Interchangeable with "eyrie," "historical nest," or simply "nest."

Nesting attempt: a raptor nest used in a given season by an adult raptor pair, confirmed by: 1) eggs or nestlings in the nest, 2) eggshell fragments in the new nesting material of raptors that build nest constructs (i.e., buteos, accipiters, eagles, kites), 3) an adult soft- or hard-incubating eggs on a nest or scrape. Includes successful nests and nest failures.

Nesting pair: a pair of raptors that has been confirmed nesting in a specific territory based on at least one of the following: 1) incubation of eggs at a nest, 2) incubation of hatchlings at a nest, 3) feeding of hatchlings / nestlings at a nest, 4) feeding of fledglings at / near a nest.

Nestling: young raptor in nest, older than a hatchling and not yet fledged.

Non-core areas: encompass all historical prairie falcon territories not included within core areas, i.e., where there is no possibility of climbing impacts and there are no historical climbing routes.

Observation Point: see Watch Spot

Occiput: posterior portion of the crown. Also known as the "hird head."

Occupancy: any territory containing at least one adult prairie falcon engaged in nest defense. Presence of a territorial prairie falcon on any of the three surveys confirms occupancy, and lack of presence after three surveys confirms lack of occupancy. Evidence of a pair with a nest indicates Territorial Occupancy.

Primaries: the outermost and longest flight feathers on a bird's wing. Members of the Order Falconiformes have ten primaries.

Productivity: used synonymously with fecundity. The number of raptor young that reach the minimum acceptable age for assessing success. We report both the number chicks that hatch per nest and the number of raptors that fledge to allow comparison with other studies.

Post-fledglings: see "fledged young."

Rectrices: tail feathers.

Remiges: large feathers of the wing, the primaries, and secondaries.

Roost: a perch or nest where raptors return to rest or sleep. Also see "sleep-roost."

Scapulars: a group of feathers on the shoulder, along the side of the back.

Scrape: a type of nest, common to prairie and peregrine falcons, shaped as a bowl-like shallow depression in soil or rocky material; site where falcons, owls, and New World vultures (species that do not construct nests) lay eggs; the depression in substrate (rotting wood chips, old pellets, dust, sand, or gravel) where eggs are deposited.

Second-year: a raptor in its second year, characterized by second-year feather development, plumage, coloration. Also called "yearling" and "sub-adult."

Secondaries: large flight feathers located in a series along the rear edge of the wing, immediately inward from the primaries.

Sleep-roost: a roost in an occupied territory that a raptor will return to near dusk to perch and sleep at during the night.

Soft incubation: an adult raptor consistently on eggs at a nest in incubation posture with periods of 20 or more consecutive minutes not on eggs between each period incubating eggs.

Stoop: a raptor descending quickly in flight by folding its wings forward, bringing its talons forward, and diving steeply. Used as a hunting technique – especially by peregrine falcons – and as a defensive behavior by a territorial raptor against threatening animals, often other raptors but also including people and potential predators.

Sub-adult: a raptor characterized by sub-adult feather development, plumage, coloration. Refers to all raptors not termed juvenile or adult birds. For most raptors, this refers to second-year birds, but can include third-year birds for golden and bald eagles.

Successful nest: nest that produces at least 1 confirmed fledgling.

Supercilliary region: area below the boundary of the forehead and the crown; the area above the eye.

Territorial occupancy: any territory containing one or more adults engaged in courtship or reproductive activity, nest defense, nest affinity, or containing eggs, young, or any field sign indicating that eggs were laid, or young were present. Evidence for territorial occupancy can include: 1) eggs or nestlings in the nest, 2) eggshell fragments in the new nesting material of raptors that build nest constructs, 3) an adult on the nest in incubation posture or an adult in a scrape for at least 1 hour (this can be a combination of both adults' time as long as the scrape has been under constant surveillance), 4) fledged young in the immediate area of the nest, or 5) field sign (fresh whitewash, decorated nests, etc.).

Territorial pair: a pair of raptors that has been confirmed occupying a territory based on at least 1 of the following: 1) an adult raptor pair actively defending and sleep-roosting in a territory, 2) adults engaged in courtship or reproductive activity, nest defense, or nest affinity, 3) incubation of hatchlings at a nest, 3) feeding of hatchlings / nestlings at a nest, 4) feeding of fledglings at / near a nest. Territorial pairs of raptors may occupy a territory throughout a season without nesting, may have a nest attempt that fails, or may abandon a territory.

Territory: within this protocol, territory refers to breeding territory. This is an area that contains, or historically contained, one or more nests (or scrapes) within the home range of a mated raptor pair; a confined locality where nests are found, usually in successive years, and where no more than one pair of a given species is known to have bred at one time. The definition does not encompass feeding areas much of which is outside of the park and is not synonymous with nest site.

Thermoregulation: the ability of an organism to keep its body temperature within certain boundaries, even when the surrounding temperature is very different. This process is also known as homeostasis.

Tiercel: a male raptor.

Wailing: a call made by prairie and peregrine falcons during copulations, in courtship, greetings, nest switches, food exchanges, and during territorial defense. Also described as "kak-kakking." Scold and alarm calls are characterized by more rapid, insistent, and harsh wailing; nestling begging calls are often ragged, rattling, and insistent wails.

Watch Spot: a location chosen by a raptor raptor technician / park biologist to observe raptor presence, behavior, and nests from. Also called an "observation point."

8 - Literature Cited

Becker, D. M., and I. J. Ball. 1981. Impacts of surface mining on prairie falcons: recommendations for monitoring and mitigation. Montana Cooperative Wildlife Research Unit, Montana State University, Missoula, MT.

Bednarz, J. C. 1984. Effect of mining and blasting on breeding prairie falcon (*Falco mexicanus*) occupancy in the Caballo Mountains. New Mexico Raptor Research 18:16–19.

Bennetts, R. E., J. E. Gross, K. Cahill, C. McIntyre, B. Bingham, A. Hubbard, L. Cameron, and S. L. Carter. Linking monitoring to management and planning: assessment points as a generalized approach. George Wright Forum 24 (2): 59-77.

Bildstein, K. L., and K. Meyer. 2000. Sharp-shinned Hawk (*Accipiter striatus*). No. 482 *in* A. Poole and F. Gill, editors. The Birds of North America. The Birds of North America, Inc., Philadelphia, PA.

Bloom, P. H. 1994. The biology and current status of the long-eared owl in coastal southern California. Bulletin Southern California Academy of Science 93:1–12.

Bond, R. M. 1946. The peregrine populations of western North America. Condor 48:101–116.

Boyce, D. A., Jr. 1982. Prairie falcon fledgling productivity in the Mojave Desert, California. Thesis. Humboldt State University, Arcata, CA.

Brown, D. E. 1982. Madrean evergreen woodland. Pages 59–65 *in* Brown, D. E. editor. Biotic communities of the American southwest-United States and Mexico. Desert Plants 4:1–342.

Brown J. S., B. P. Kotler, R. J. Smith and W. O. Wirtz II. 1988. The effects of owl predation on the foraging behavior of heteromyid rodents. Oecologia 76:408–415.

Buranek, S. 2006. Pinnacles prairie falcon home range and habitat analysis. Thesis. California State Univeristy, Sacramento, CA.

Buhl-Mortensen, L. 1996. Type II statistical errors in environmental science and the precautionary principle. Marine Pollution Bulletin 32:528–531.

Cade, T. J., J. H. Enderson, and J. Linthicum. 1996. Guide to management of peregrine falcons at the eyrie. The Peregrine Fund, Inc., Boise, ID.

California Department of Fish and Game. 2008. Special animals (865 taxa). California Department of Fish and Game, Biogeographic Data Branch, California Natural Diversity Database, Sacramento, CA. Available online: http://www.dfg.ca.gov/biogeodata/cnddb/pdfs/SPAnimals.pdf (accessed 1 September 2008).

Cohen, J. 1988. *Statistical Power Analysis for the Behavioral Sciences* (2nd ed.), New York: Academic Press.

Croll, D. A., J. L. Maron, J. A. Estes, E. M. Danner, and G. V. Byrd. 2005. Introduced predators transform subarctic islands from grassland to tundra. Science 307:1959–1961.

Delannoy, C. A., and A. Cruz. 1988. Breeding biology of the Puerto Rican sharp-shinned hawk (*Accipiter striatus venator*). Auk 105:649–662.

Dunk, J. R. 1995. White-tailed kite (*Elanus leucurus*). No. 178 *in* A. Poole and F. Gill, editors. The Birds of North America. The Academy of Natural Sciences, Philadelphia, and The American Ornithologists' Union, Washington, D.C.

Ellis, D. H. 1973. Behavior of the golden eagle: an ontogenic study. Dissertation. University of Montana, Missoula, MT.

Emmons, G. 2006. Raptor breeding season report for Pinnacles National Monument – 2006. Unpublished report. National Park Service, San Francisco Bay Area Network Inventory and Monitoring Program, San Francisco, CA.

Fesnock, A. 1993. Seasonal duties of the raptor technician. Unpublished. Pinnacles National Monument, Paicines, CA.

Fraser, J. D., L. D. Frenzel, J. E. Mathisen, F. Martin, and M. E. Shough. 1983. Scheduling bald eagle reproduction surveys. Wildlife Society Bulletin 11:13–16.

Fuller, M. R., and J. A. Mosher. 1981. Methods of detecting and counting raptors: a review. Studies in Avian Biology 6:235–246.

Fyfe, R. W., and R. R. Olendorff. 1976. Minimizing the dangers of nesting studies to raptors and other sensitive species. Canadian Wildlife Serv. Occas. Pap. 23:1–17.

Gibbs, J. P., S. Droege, and P. Eagle. 1998. Monitoring populations of plants and animals. *BioScience* 48:935–940.

Haemig, P. D. 2001. Symbiotic nesting of birds with formidable animals: a review with applications to biodiversity conservation. Biodiversity Conservation 10:527–540.

Harmata, A. R., J. E. Durr, and H. Geduldig. 1978. Home range, activity patterns and habitat use of prairie falcons nesting in the Mojave Desert. Unpublished report to the U.S. Department of the Interior, Bureau of Land Management, Riverside, CA.

Hickey, J. J. 1942. Eastern population of the duck hawk. Auk 59:176–204.

Hickey, J. J. 1969. Peregrine falcon populations: their biology and decline. University of Wisconsin Press, Madison, WI.

Holthuijzen, A. M. A., W. G. Eastland, A. R. Ansell, M. N. Kochert, R. D. Williams, and L. S. Young. 1990. Effects of blasting on behavior and productivity of nesting prairie falcons. Wildlife Society Bulletin 18:270–281.

Jaksic, F. M., P. Feinsinger, and J. E. Jimenez. 1996. Ecological redundancy and long-term dynamics of vertebrate predators in semiarid Chile. Conservation Biology 10:252–262.

Kochert, M. N., K. Steenhof, L. B. Carpenter, and J. M. Marzluff. 1999. Effects of fire on golden eagle territory occupancy and reproductive success. Journal of Wildlife Management 63:773–780.

Kochert, M. N., K. Steenhof, C. L. McIntyre, and E. H. Craig. 2002. Golden eagle (*Aquila chrysaetos*). No. 684 *in* A. Poole and F. Gill, editors. The Birds of North America. The Birds of North America, Inc., Philadelphia, PA.

Lundberg, J. and F. Moberg. 2003. Mobile link organisms and ecosystem functioning: implications for ecosystem resilience and management. Ecosystems 6:87–98.

MacDonald, T. L. 2003. Review of Environmental Monitoring Methods: Survey Designs. Environmental Monitoring and Assessment **85**:277-292.

MacKenzie, D. I., J. D. Nichols, J. A. Royle, K. H. Pollock, L. L. Bailey, J. E. Hines. 2006. Occupancy Estimation and Modeling: Inferring Patterns and Dynamics of Species Occurrence. Elsevier Academic Press. Burlington.

Mapstone, B. D. 1995. Scalable decision rules for environmental impact studies: effect size, Type I, and Type II errors. *Ecological Applications* 5:401–410.

Marks, J. S. 1986. Nest-site characteristics and reproductive success of long-eared owls in southwestern Idaho. Wilson Bulletin 98:547–560.

Marshall Jr., J. T. 1957. Birds of the pine-oak woodland in southern Arizona and adjacent Mexico. Pacific Coast Avifauna 32:1–125.

Marti, C. D. and J. S. Marks. 1989. Medium-sized owls. Pages 124–133 *in* B. G. Pendleton, editor. Proceedings of the Western Raptor Management Symposium and Workshop. National Wildlife Federation, Science and Technical Series No. 12.

Marzluff, J. M., M. S. Vekasy, and C. Coody. 1994. Comparative accuracy of aerial and ground telemetry locations of foraging raptors. Condor 96:447–454.

Marzluff, J. M., B. A. Kimsey, L. S. Schueck, M. E. McFadzen, M. S. Vekasy, and J. C. Bednarz. 1997. The influence of habitat, prey abundance, sex, and breeding success on the ranging behavior of prairie falcons. Condor 99:567–584.

Mazur, K. M. and P. C. James. 2000. Barred owl (*Strix varia*). No. 508 *in* A. Poole and F. Gill, editors. The Birds of North America. The Birds of North America, Inc., Philadelphia, PA.

McFadzen, M.E., and J. M. Marzluff. 1996. Mortality of prairie falcons during the fledging dependence period. Condor 98:791–800.

Meyer, K. D. 1995. Swallow-tailed kite (*Elanoides forficatus*). No. 138 *in* A. Poole and F. Gill, editors. The Birds of North America. The Academy of Natural Sciences, Philadelphia, and The American Ornithologists' Union, Washington, D.C.

Millenium Ecosystem Assessment. 2005. Ecosystems and human well-being: synthesis. Island Press, Washington, D.C.

Mitani, J. C., W. Sanders, J. Lwanga, and T. Windfelder. 2001. Predatory behavior of crowned-hawk eagles in the in Kibale National Park, Uganda. Behavioral Ecology and Sociobiology 49:187–195.

Newton, I. 1979. Population ecology of raptors. Buteo Books, Shipman, VA.

Newton, I. 1990. Birds of prey. Facts on File, Inc., New York, NY.

Ogden, V. T., and M. G. Hornocker. 1977. Nesting density and success of prairie falcons in southwestern Idaho. Journal of Wildlife Management 41:1–11.

Olsen, P., and J. Olsen. 1978. Alleviating the impact of human disturbance on the breeding peregrine falcon I. Corella 2(1):1–7.

Olsen, J., and P. Olsen. 1980. Alleviating the impact of human disturbance on the breeding Peregrine Falcon II. Public and recreational lands. Corella 4(3):54–57.

Parrish, J. K., M. Marvier, and R. T. Paine. 2001 Direct and indirect effects: interactions between bald eagles and common murres. Ecological Applications 11:1858–1869.

Platt, S. W. 1974. Breeding status and distribution of the prairie falcon in northern New Mexico. Thesis. Oklahoma State University, Stillwate, OK.

Porter, R. D., M. A. Jenkins, and A. L. Ganski. 1987. Working bibliography of the peregrine falcon. National Wildlife Federation, Science and Technical Series, No. 9.

Preisser, E. L., D. I. Bolnick, and M. F. Benard. 2005. Scared to death? Behavioral effects dominate predator–prey interactions. Ecology 86:501–509.

Press, D. T. 2005. Data management plan for the San Francisco Bay Area Network Inventory and Monitoring Program. U. S. Department of the Interior, National Park Service, San Francisco, CA.

Ralph, C. J., G. R. Geupel, P. Pyle, T. E. Martin, and D. F. DeSante. 1993. Handbook of field methods for monitoring landbirds. General Technical Report PSW-GTR-144. U. S. Forest Service, Pacific Southwest Research Station, Albany, CA.

Rechtin, J. A. 1992. Raptor nesting at Pinnacles National Monument: 1984–1992. Pinnacles National Monument, Paicines, CA.

Rechtin, J., and T. Leatherman. 1992. Directions for taking raptor observations. Unpublished report. Pinnacles National Monument, Paicines, CA.

Roemer, G. W., C. J. Donlan, and F. Courchamp. 2002. Golden eagles, feral pigs and insular carnivores: how exotic species turn native predators into prey. Proceedings of the National Academy of Sciences 99(2):791–796.

Rubine, D. 1995. Climber's guide to Pinnacles National Monument, 2nd edition. Chockstone Press, Inc. Evergreen, CO.

Scott, T. A. 1985. Human impacts on the golden eagle population of San Diego County. Thesis. San Diego State University, San Diego, CA.

Sekercioglu, C. H. 2006a. Ecological significance of bird populations. Handbook of the Birds of the World. 11:3–39.

Sekercioglu, C. H. 2006b. Increasing awareness of avian ecological function. Trends in Ecology and Evolution. 21(8):464–471.

Sitter, G. 1983. Feeding activity and behavior of prairie falcons in the Snake River Birds of Prey Natural Area in southwestern Idaho. Thesis. University of Idaho, Moscow, ID.

Smith, J. P., and A. Hutchins. 2006. Northeast Nevada nest survey 2005. Hawkwatch International, Inc., Salt Lake City, Utah.

Sodhi, N. S., A. Didiuk, and L. W. Oliphant. 1990. Differences in bird abundance in relation to proximity of merlin nests. Canadian Journal of Zoology 68:852–854.

Squires, J. R. and R. T. Reynolds. 1997. Northern goshawk (*Accipiter gentilis*). No. 298 *in* A. Poole and F. Gill, editors. The Birds of North America. The Academy of Natural Sciences, Philadelphia, PA, and The American Ornithologists' Union, Washington, D.C.

Starcevich, L. A. and K. Steinhorst. 2010. Analysis of Power to Detect Trends in Occupancy and Fecundity in Prairie Falcon and Spotted Owl Populations. Unpublished report to San Francisco Bay Area Network of the Inventory and Monitoring Program, National Park Service, Golden Gate National Recreation Area, Sausalito, CA.

Steenhof, K. 1987. Assessing raptor reproductive success and productivity. Pages 157–170 *in* B. A. Giron Pendleton, B. A. Milsap, K. W. Cline, and D. M. Bird, editors. Raptor Management Techniques Manual. National Wildlife Federation, Washington, D.C.

Steenhof, K. 1998. Prairie falcon (*Falco mexicanus*). No. 346 *in* A. Poole and F. Gill, editors. The Birds of North America. The Birds of North America, Inc., Philadelphia, PA.

Steenhof, K., M. N. Kochert, and T. L. McDonald. 1997. Interactive effects of prey and weather on golden eagle reproduction. Journal of Animal Ecology 66:350–362.

Steenhof, K., M. N. Kochert, L. B. Carpenter, and R. N. Lehman. 1999. Long-term prairie falcon population changes in relation to prey abundance, weather, land uses, and habitat conditions. Condor 101:28–41.

Steidl, R. J., K. D. Kozie, G. J. Dodge, T. Pehovski, and E. R. Hogan. 1993. Effects of human activity on breeding behavior of golden eagles in Wrangell-St. Elias National Park and Preserve: a preliminary assessment. WRST Research and Resource Management Report no. 93-3. National Park Service, Wrangell-St. Elias National Park and Preserve, Copper Center, AK.

Stiles, F. G. 1985. On the role of birds in the dynamics of neotropical forests. Pages 49–59 *in* A. W. Diamond and T. E. Lovejoy, editors. Conservation of Tropical Forest Birds. International Council for Bird Preservation, Cambridge, UK.

Suter, G. W., and J. L. Joness. 1981. Criteria for golden eagle, ferruginous hawk, and prairie falcon nest site protection. Raptor Research 15:12–18.

U.S. Department of the Interior. 1979. Snake River birds of prey special research report to the Secretary of the Interior. U.S. Bureau of Land Management, Boise, ID.

U.S. Fish and Wildlife Service. 1984. American peregrine falcon rocky mountain/southwest population recovery plan (Rocky Mountain/Southwest population). U.S. Fish and Wildlife Service, Denver, CO.

Urquhart, N. S., and T. M. Kincaid. 1999. Trend detection in repeated surveys of ecological responses. Journal of Agricultural, Biological, and Environmental Statistics 4:404-414.

Watson, J. 1997. The golden eagle. 1st edition. T and A. D. Poyser Ltd, London, U.K.

White, C. M., N. J. Clum, T. J. Cade, and W. G. Hunt. 2002. Peregrine falcon (*Falco peregrinus*). No. 660 *in* A. Poole, editor. The Birds of North America Online. Cornell Laboratory of Ornithology, Ithaca, NY. Retrieved from The Birds of North American Online database: http://bna.birds.cornell.edu/BNA/account/Peregrine_Falcon/ (accessed on 1 September 2008).

Appendix A. Analysis of power to detect trends in occupancy and fecundity in prairie falcon and spotted owl populations

**San Francisco Bay Area Network
of the
National Park Service**

Authors:
Leigh Ann Harrod Starcevich
Kirk Steinhorst

March 2010

In Partial Fulfillment of
Contract Number J8W07060004
Contractor: Kirk Steinhorst, University of Idaho
Subcontractor: Leigh Ann Harrod Starcevich
PO Box 1032
Corvallis, OR 97339
lah@peak.org

TABLE OF CONTENTS

ACKNOWLEDGMENTS

The authors would like to thank Marcus Koenen, Dave Press, Bill Merkle, and Gavin Emmons of the San Francisco Area Network for providing helpful background for this analysis and Kathryn M. Irvine for her help with occupancy modeling.

1. INTRODUCTION

The San Francisco Bay Area Network (SFAN) of the National Park Service (NPS) has identified prairie falcon and spotted owl populations as two of the network's Vital Signs for long-term monitoring. Specifically, trends in occupancy and fecundity will be monitored so that detrimental changes in the population can be identified to inform timely management decisions. The analysis approaches for measures of occupancy and fecundity are first discussed, and then power to detect trends in occupancy and fecundity is computed for all metrics of interest for the two species.

2. GENERAL ANALYSIS APPROACH

The models for both occupancy and fecundity incorporate zero inflation. For occupancy analysis, extra zeroes may result from imperfect detection. When measuring fecundity, counts of hatchlings or fledglings might be subject to zeroes from nest failures due to non-nesting pairs, predation, or environmental factors. Analysis methods for zero-inflation apply mixture models that combine one distribution for the extra zeroes and another distribution for the remaining zeroes and non-zero outcomes so that measures of occupancy and fecundity can be accurately estimated (MacKenzie et al. 2006). The number of detections for occupancy analysis and the number of hatchlings or fledglings for fecundity analysis are modeled as zero-inflated binomial random variables.

2.1 Occupancy and trend modeling

Let y_{ijk} be the outcome for site i, year j, and visit k, and let y_{ijk} take a value of 1 if a prairie falcon is detected and 0 otherwise. Let y_{ijk} be the number of detections made at site i and year j during the kth visit. The zero-inflated binomial distribution is expressed as:

$$P\left(Y = y_{ijk}\right) = \pi_{ij} p_{ij}^{y_{ijk}} \left(1 - p_{ij}\right)^{1 - y_{ijk}} + \left(1 - \pi_{ij}\right) I\left(y_{ijk} = 0\right),$$

where π_j is the occupancy rate in year j and p_{ij} is the detection rate for site i and year j. Assume that there are S sites, T years, and K visits to a site each year. Define the indicator function as $I\left(y_{ij} = 0\right)$ as 1 when $y_{ij} = 0$ and 0 otherwise. This model assumes an equal number of visits to a site within a year, but K can vary among sites or among years.

Occupancy (π) is modeled with logistic regression as a function of related covariates:

$$\log\left(\frac{\pi_{ij}}{1 - \pi_{ij}}\right) = \gamma_0 + \gamma_1 x_{ij},$$

where x_{ij} represents a covariate for the ith site and the jth year. Multiple site-level or year-level covariates may be incorporated. To test for linear trend in the logged odds ratio of occupancy, the year covariate should be included as a predictor in the occupancy model. The probability of zero inflation (p) is simultaneously estimated by logistic regression:

$$\log\left(\frac{p_{ij}}{1-p_{ij}}\right) = \beta_0 + \beta'_1 x_{ijk},$$

where x_{ijk} represents a covariate collected at the ith site and k^{th} visit during the jth year.

The implicit dynamics occupancy model is assumed for this analysis. In contrast to the explicit dynamics model, estimates of colonization and local extinction are not explicitly measured in the implicit dynamics model (MacKenzie et al. 2006). The net effect of extinction and colonization rates on occupancy is monitored rather than estimating the parameters separately since monitoring net change over time is the primary goal.

Maximum likelihood is used to estimate the regression coefficients from the models for occupancy and detection rates. Occupancy can be modeled at the site-by-year level so predictors should be collected at the site level, year level, or site-by-year level. Detection probabilities are allowed to vary at each visit for each site and year, so covariates are often environmental covariates that vary from visit to visit (MacKenzie et al. 2006). However, if detection rates are also changing over time, a model that includes a year covariate may be needed for accurate occupancy estimation. Model selection is conducted using the Akaike Information Criterion (AIC). Model output is examined to be certain that valid variance estimates are obtained. When valid estimates of the variance cannot be acquired for the model with the lowest AIC, then the model with the lowest AIC and valid variance is used.

2.2 Fecundity and trend modeling

Fecundity is monitored with counts of hatchlings or fledglings observed at each nest. These outcomes are also modeled with the zero-inflated binomial model. Let y_{ij} be the number of hatchlings or fledglings detected in occupied site i and year j. Let n be the number of occupied sites and T be the number of years monitored for fecundity. The probability mass function of Y is:

$$P\left(Y = y_{ij}\right) = \pi_{ij}\binom{M}{y_{ij}} p_{ij}^{\,y_{ij}}\left(1-p_{ij}\right)^{M-y_{ij}} + \left(1-\pi_{ij}\right)I\left(y_{ij} = 0\right),$$

where π_{ij} is the probability that an extra 0 is **not** observed at site i in year j, p_{ij} is the probability of a hatchling/fledgling at site i in year j, M is the maximum number of hatchlings/fledglings seen in any nest, and $I(y_{ij} = 0)$ is 1 when $y_{ij} = 0$ and is 0 otherwise. Maximum likelihood estimation is used to obtain estimates of the regression coefficients in each model, and the invariance property of maximum likelihood estimates is used to obtain estimates of π_{ij} and p_{ij}.

To test for trend in fecundity, the year covariate is included as a predictor in the binomial probability model and then tested for significance with a likelihood ratio test. In contrast to the occupancy analysis, fecundity inference is made on the change in p_{ij} over time.

2.3 Power approach

Power is often calculated assuming large-sample properties for hypothesis tests of significance. However, the assumptions necessary for assuming asymptotic normality are extensive and often difficult to verify (Sumathi and Aruna Rao, 2009). Ridout et al. (2001) observed that the normal approximation to the score test underestimates the true test size for testing the significance of the dispersion parameter when comparing the zero-inflated negative binomial and zero-inflated Poisson distributions. Jung et al. (2005) corrected this problem with a parametric bootstrapping approach to significance testing, which provided uniformly higher power. For both prairie falcon and spotted owl monitoring, trend is tested with the likelihood ratio test, which demonstrates power equal to or higher than that provided by the Wald test (Lyles et al. 2006).

Model selection for occupancy and fecundity is conducted using the pilot data for prairie falcons and spotted owls. In each case, the model with the lowest AIC score with a valid variance-covariance matrix is used in the power analysis. In all four cases, power is computed via a parametric bootstrap. For each bootstrap sample, the likelihood ratio test of trend is conducted by applying the selected model with and without the term for trend. Power is calculated as the proportion of times that the null hypothesis is rejected for the one-sided alternative hypothesis of decreasing trend, i.e.,

$$H_o : \beta = 0 \text{ vs. } H_a : \beta < 0 .$$

Power must be approximated assuming that tests of trend are conducted at a specific Type I error rate. The Type I error rate, designated as α, is the probability of rejecting a true null hypothesis. For two-sided tests of trend, a Type I error would mean that the population was found to be changing when it was not. A Type II error occurs by failing to reject a false null hypothesis and thus concluding no change has occurred. For long-term monitoring, the cost of a Type I error may be far less than the cost of a Type II error. Mistakenly rejecting a true null hypothesis (Type I error) may trigger a management conservation action that is not actually needed. However, failing to detect a significant trend may have deleterious effects that cannot be reversed by the time the trend is actually detected. A conservative approach is to use a larger α value for higher power and reduced probability of a Type II error (Buhl-Mortensen 1996; Gibbs, et al. 1998; Mapstone 1995). For this power analysis, an α value of 0.20 is used. Power does not fall below the α value assumed for the trend test.

2.4 Revisit designs

Revisit designs specify the schedule of sites visitations by year for the duration of the monitoring period. Revisit design allow balance over space and time of available survey effort. The notation of McDonald (2003) is used to describe the revisit designs.

The notation employs a string of numbers, dashes, and commas to identify the revisit design among panels. The numbers in odd-numbered positions will designate the number of consecutive visits to a panel before it rotates out of the revisit schedule. Digits in the even-numbered positions indicate the number of sampling occasions that the panel will not be revisited. Therefore, a revisit schedule of [1-0] indicates that the panel will be revisited each year and never rotated out of the schedule. This revisit schedule is equivalent to taking a random sample of sites and visiting them every year. The [1-n] revisit design represents a sampling design in which independent random samples are taken every year. A [2-2] revisit design consists of one panel visited for two consecutive years and then rested for two consecutive years before beginning the cycle again. Differing revisit schedules among panels are indicated by separating the digits in parentheses by commas within the brackets. For example, a revisit schedule of [(1-0), (1-3)] indicates that the revisit design includes an annual panel that is revisited every year and four panels that are visited for one year then not visited for the following three years before being rotated back into the design.

A random site effect may be incorporated in the occupancy or detection model to account for variation among sites. However, implementing the appropriate correlation structure in a mixed model approach may be problematic with maximum likelihood estimation (MacKenzie et al. 2006). Incorporating numerous fixed site effects may exhaust available degrees of freedom making variance estimates unreliable and trend testing inaccurate. Without fixed or random site effects, the data are treated as if collected from a [1-n] revisit design. This revisit design has the lowest power for trend detection (Urquhart and Kincaid, 1999), so power results are conservative. Since site effects are difficult to incorporate, MacKenzie et al. (2006) suggest using a [1-0] design so that unexplained variation among sites is minimized for more accurate tests of trend. Incorporating relevant site-level covariates into the occupancy model will also help explain differences in occupancy from site-to-site.

3. PRAIRIE FALCON POWER ANALYSES

SFAN, in cooperation with Pinnacles National Monument (PINN), has monitored the occupancy rate and fecundity measures of the prairie falcon population in PINN since 1984. SFAN personnel are interested in monitoring trends in occupancy and fecundity measures. This section will address the power to detect changes in prairie falcon occupancy and fecundity measurements over time.

3.1 Survey design

The target population includes 36 territories historically used by prairie falcon in PINN. Of the 36 territories in the target population, 18 of these territories fall into the "core" area. The core area consists of territories that are more accessible to climbers and hikers. These areas have been surveyed more consistently and frequently over the last 22 years to assess hiking/climbing pressure during the breeding season. Eighteen non-core areas were identified and added to the sample over time. Due to the added monitoring importance of the core areas, the core and non-core areas will be treated as separate strata with core territories censused annually. Depending on survey resources and the results of the power analysis, the non-core territories will be either censused or allocated to a set of panels that are visited on an alternating cycle.

Sites are visited at least 3 times each year with visits lasting 1 to 4 hours. At least 3 visits to a site are needed to determine that a site is unoccupied, and visits are spaced 21 to 28 days apart. In sites where prairie falcon detections are made, territorial occupancy is assessed by examining the behavior of each detected prairie falcon. Territorial behavior is verified by observing courtship or reproductive behavior or by evidence of offspring.

Pilot data collected since 1984 are available with a more consistent effort made since 2002. Detections from Ball Pinnacle and Central High Peaks were excluded because these territories are near other historic territories and are not considered independent territories. Some survey records for territories in which no detections were made were omitted from the database prior to the 2008 survey, potentially causing invalid inference on occupancy and detection rates from the incomplete data set. For this reason, only the 2008 and 2009 data are used for the power analysis. This database problem does not affect the fecundity data set because the subset of pair-occupied sites is the target population for fecundity monitoring. Fecundity monitoring data were collected from 2002 to 2009. While fecundity data are available since 1984, the data collected since 2002 represent the current methodology and are thought to be more consistent.

SFAN is interested in approximating the power to detect trends in occupancy and fecundity measures. For a Type I error rate of 0.2, the power to detect a 50% decline in each indicator of interest over a 10-year period in a one-sided alternative hypothesis is examined for several sample sizes and revisit designs.

3.2 Occupancy analysis

The definition of occupancy requires a verification of territorial behavior. A prairie falcon detection does not necessarily imply that occupancy has been established. Designation of site occupancy requires multiple site visits within a year and evidence of territorial behavior. To estimate occupancy according to the SFAN definition of occupancy, only detections verifying territorial behavior should be used. Detection probabilities from this analysis would reflect the detection of an individual or pair displaying territorial behavior. However, the current data set reflects all detections regardless of behavior. Therefore, occupancy may be overestimated in this analysis. Data analysis may be improved by recording an indicator that the detection provides proof of territorial occupancy. This field could be recorded as a 0/1 binary field rather than a descriptive field for easier data analysis.

The pilot data are examined to determine if the estimated detection rates for prairie falcon are substantially less than one, indicating that occupancy estimates should be calculated assuming imperfect detection. In the next section, the occupancy analysis approach and concurrent estimation of trend over time are discussed. All occupancy estimates relate to pair occupancy since no single prairie falcons were observed in 2008 or 2009.

3.2.1 Evaluation of detection probabilities

Maximum likelihood estimation was used to obtain estimates of regression coefficients for models of occupancy and detection rates. Occupancy models were based on a site-level covariate (an indicator for core area) and the survey year. Detection models were based on covariates collected within each site and year such as month, high temperature, low temperature, average wind speed, cloud cover, and level of precipitation. The occupancy model selected from the modeling exercise contained covariates for the year and core area inclusion. The three detection models with the lowest AIC are given in Table 3.1. The lowest detection probabilities from the first model were obtained for the relatively-few PRFA surveys conducted when precipitation was present. Because the AIC for the month-only detection model is only slightly larger, this more parsimonious model is used for model stability.

Table 3.1: Best detection models from 2008-2009 pilot data

Detection model variables	AIC	Range of estimated detection rates	2008 estimated occupancy rate (SE)	2009 estimated occupancy rate (SE)
Hi_TempF, CCPct, Precip_Code	518.31	0.3011 – 0.6965	0.9271 (0.1020)	1.0000 (0.0031)
Month, Precip_Code	519.84	0.3281 – 0.6511	0.8788 (0.0957)	1.0000 (0.0016)
Month	520.27	0.3305 – 0.6513	0.8787 (0.0956)	1.0000 (0.0010)

Plotting the estimated detection probabilities against the month predictor (Figure 3.1), one may observe that detection probabilities for PRFA are highest later in the season. A *t*-test of the two-sided hypothesis that the mean detection rate is equal to 1 is highly significant (p-value < 0.0001). There is no evidence that PRFA detection probabilities are so high as to warrant conducting a trend analysis that assumes perfect detectability. Therefore, the zero-inflated Bernoulli distribution is assumed.

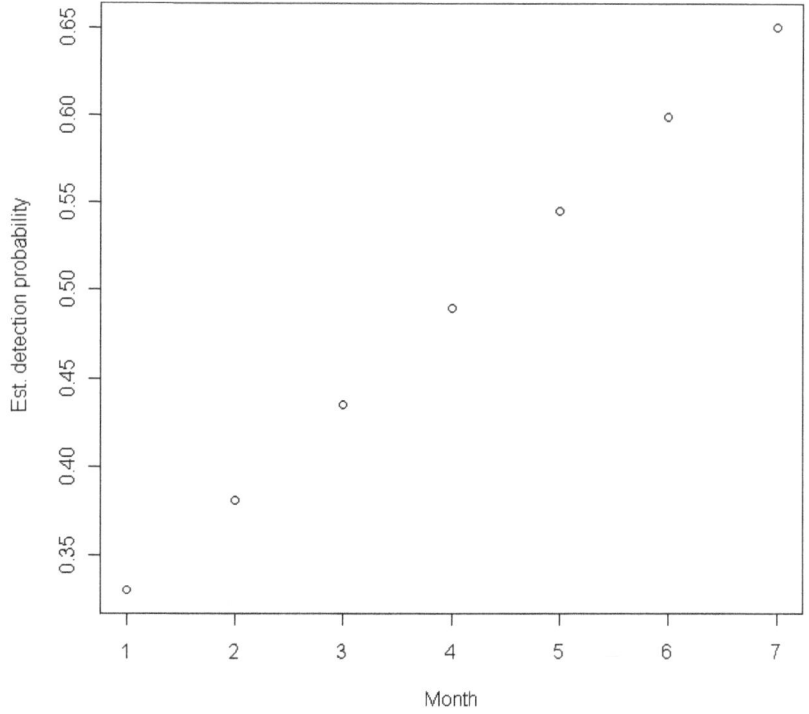

Figure 3.1: Estimated detection probabilities by month

3.2.2 Power analysis

The power analysis is conducted using the parametric bootstrapping approach. The models for occupancy and detection obtained from the pilot data are used. The month covariate is randomly selected from the pilot data so that months in which prairie falcon surveys are more common will occur more frequently in the bootstrap samples.

Power is examined for a range of sample sizes that are visited using several revisit designs. Figures 3.2 through 3.5 provide illustrations of several possible revisit designs for a range of annual sample sizes. For each revisit design, the set of core territories is visited annually and all territories are visited at least once over the course of the revisit cycle. Notice that, for the [(1-0), (1-4)] revisit design, 10 years are required to obtain complete replication at all territories. For the [(1-0), (1-1)] design, all sites are visited at least twice in four survey years. When the [1-0] revisit design is used, all sites are visited annually and a complete replicate is obtained after the second survey year.

An issue that arose in the occupancy modeling exercise is the difficulty in obtaining stable maximum likelihood estimates from occupancy and detection models that incorporate an effect for the territory. Fixed effects for each site require considerable degrees of freedom that can result in erroneous variance estimation. Incorporating a random effect into the detection model for a heterogeneous detection probability model generated occupancy estimates very close to 1 in every case. Furthermore, occupancy and detection models with any complexity generally produced Hessian matrices that were not positive-definite, so standard errors for trend estimation could be wrong. Since neither a fixed nor a random effect for territory can be incorporated into the models, the sample is treated as if were collected in a [1-n] design. The revisit designs cannot be distinguished from another because the benefits of sampling the same sites annually cannot be integrated into the model. However, the [1-n] revisit design has lowest power for trend detection, so the power results provided here are conservative.

MacKenzie et al. (2006) suggest that the heterogeneous detection probability model, while difficult to implement in a maximum likelihood setting, may be conducted with a Bayesian approach. When incorporating a fixed or random site effect is not possible, including site-level covariates that are related to occupancy will help explain site-to-site differences in occupancy estimates. Unexplained site-to-site variation is included in the residual error term which increases the standard error of the estimate of the trend coefficient and decreases power to detect trend.

	Year		
Panel	**Core/ non-core**	**1**	**2**
1	Core	18	18
2	Non-core	3	3
ANNUAL TOTAL		21	21

Figure 3.2: [1-0] revisit design for annual census of core sites and sample of 3 non-core sites

	Year									
Panel	**Core/ non-core**	**1**	**2**	**3**	**4**	**5**	**6**	**7**	**8**	**9**	**10**
1	Core	18	18	18	18	18	18	18	18	18	18
2	Non-core	3	3	3	3	3	3	3	3	3	3
3	Non-core	3					3				
4	Non-core		3					3			
5	Non-core			3					3		
6	Non-core				3					3	
7	Non-core					3					3
ANNUAL TOTAL		24	24	24	24	24	24	24	24	24	24

Figure 3.3: [(1-0),(1-4)] revisit design

	Year			
Panel	**Core/ non-core**	**1**	**2**	**3**	**4**
1	Core	18	18	18	18
2	Non-core	6	6	6	6
3	Non-core	6		6	
4	Non-core		6		6
ANNUAL TOTAL		30	30	30	30

Figure 3.4: [(1-0),(1-1)] revisit design

	Year		
Panel	**Core/ non-core**	**1**	**2**
1	Core	18	18
2	Non-core	18	18
ANNUAL TOTAL		36	36

Figure 3.5: [1-0] revisit design for annual census of all sites

The power to detect a 50% decline in occupancy after 10 consecutive survey years is provided in Table 3.2 for the revisit designs described in Figures 3.2 through 3.5. The [1-0] revisit design is known to have the highest power to detect trend (Urquhart and Kincaid, 1999). As discussed previously, the default revisit design is assumed to be a [1-n] design since the effect of territory cannot be explicitly modeled. Therefore, the difference among the power calculations presented in Table 3.2 is a function of annual sample size rather than an artifact of the revisit design.

Table 3.2: Power to detect occupancy trends for different sample sizes and revisit designs

Annual sample size of territories	Number of core sites surveyed annually	Number of non-core sites surveyed annually	Revisit design	Power to detect a 50% decrease after 10 consecutive survey years
18	18	0	[1-0]	0.953
21	18	3	[1-0]	0.973
24	18	6	[(1-0),(1-4)]	1.000
30	18	12	[(1-0),(1-1)]	1.000
36	18	18	[1-0]	1.000

Because the core sites must be censused each year to monitor high-use areas, the power to detect trends in non-core sites is examined separately (Table 3.3). The samples will be stratified by core and non-core areas, so trends may be estimated separately for each subpopulation. Comparisons of Tables 3.2 and 3.3 indicate that the high power to detect trends across the set of territories is largely due to the census of core sites. The pilot data did not indicate a significant difference in occupancy between core and non-core sites ($p=0.1413$). However, if future prairie falcon trends occur at different rates between core and non-core areas or if inference to the subpopulation of non-core sites is of interest, then results for trends in prairie falcon occupancy at PINN may be misleading unless at least between 9 and 12 non-core territories are surveyed each year. If historic data are corrected so that non-detections are included in the data set, the pilot data may be helpful in determining if sample sizes for non-core areas should be considered independently from the annual census of core sites.

Table 3.3: Power to detect occupancy trends for non-core sites only

Number of non-core sites surveyed annually	Revisit design	Power to detect a 50% decrease after 10 consecutive survey years
3	[1-0]	0.559
6	[1-0]	0.754
9	[1-0]	0.773
12	[1-0]	0.852

3.3 Fecundity power analysis

Fecundity will be monitored by examining trends in the binomial probability of hatchlings and fledglings. Histograms of prairie falcon hatchlings and fledglings per nest from data pooled over the years 2002 to 2009 indicate a large number of zeroes in each outcome (Figures 3.6 and 3.7, respectively). The additional zeroes may be a result of mechanisms such as imperfect detection rates, predation, or environmental factors and are accounted for using a zero-inflated binomial model. The maximum number of eggs observed in the pilot data is 5, so this is assumed to be the maximum number of hatchlings or fledglings per nest in PINN.

Assuming that the numbers of hatchlings and fledglings follow zero-inflated binomial distributions and assuming that a random sample of occupied sites are visited each year, the power to detect a 50% decline in fecundity after 10 consecutive survey years is provided for hatchlings (Table 3.4) and fledgling (Table 3.5). The results of the power analysis indicate that annual surveys of at least 10 pair-occupied sites provides power of at least 0.8 to detect a 50% decline over 10 years in hatchling or fledgling rates.

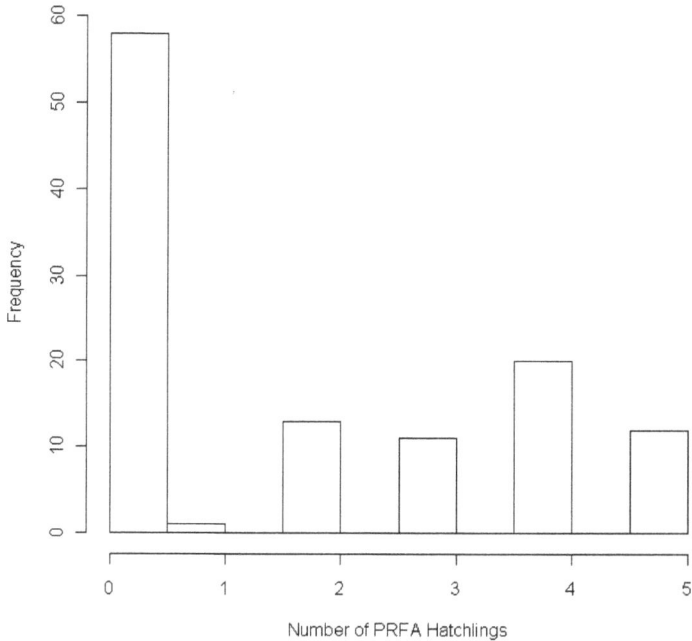

Figure 3.6: Histogram of hatchlings across years, 2002 - 2009

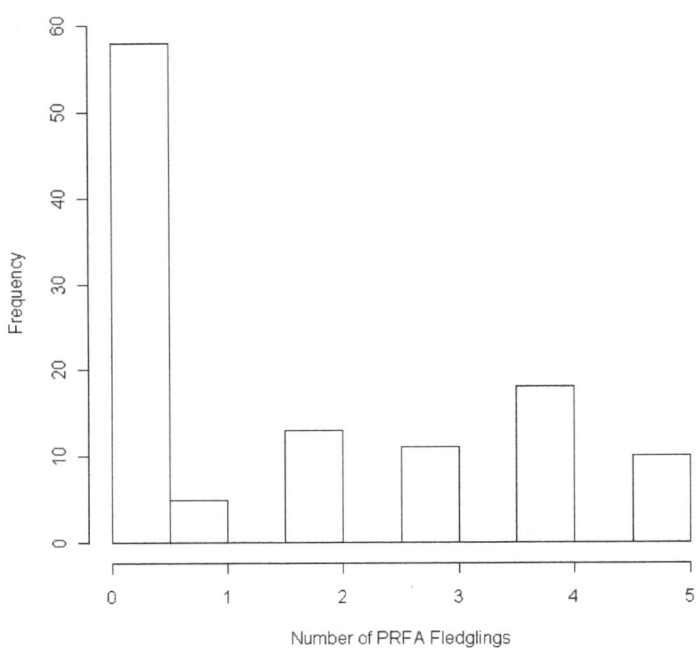

Figure 3.7: Histogram of fledglings across years, 2002 - 2009

Table 3.4: Power to detect a 50% decline in the probability of hatchlings

Annual sample size of occupied nests	Power to detect a 50% decrease after 10 years (based on 2002-2009 pilot data)
5	0.609
10	0.910
15	1.000
20	1.000
25	1.000

Table 3.5: Power to detect a 50% decline in the probability of known fledglings

Annual sample size of occupied nests	Power to detect a 50% decrease after 10 years (based on 2002-2009 pilot data)
5	0.645
10	0.922
15	0.977
20	1.000
25	1.000

Core sites are visited annually so that hiking and climbing pressure can be assessed throughout the breeding season. Given that the set of core sites is censused annually, power is examined for samples that contain all core sites and a range of non-core sites each year. For counts of both hatchlings (Table 3.6) and fledglings (Table 3.7), the power to detect trend in the binomial probability for each outcome is one. This level of power is attained even when no non-core sites are surveyed. However, if inference to non-core sites is of interest, then this subpopulation should be sampled with sufficient effort. Power to detect a 50% decline over 10 consecutive years exceeds 0.8 for as few as three sites each year for hatchlings (Table 3.8) and fledglings (Table 3.9).

Table 3.6: Power to detect trend in the binomial probability for **hatchlings** for a census of core sites and a sample of non-core sites

Annual sample size of territories	Number of core sites surveyed annually	Number of non-core sites surveyed annually	Power to detect a 50% decrease after 10 consecutive survey years
18	18	0	1.000
21	18	3	1.000
24	18	6	1.000
30	18	12	1.000
36	18	18	1.000

Table 3.7: Power to detect trend in the binomial probability for **fledglings** for a census of core sites and a sample of non-core sites

Annual sample size of territories	Number of core sites surveyed annually	Number of non-core sites surveyed annually	Power to detect a 50% decrease after 10 consecutive survey years
18	18	0	1.000
21	18	3	1.000
24	18	6	1.000
30	18	12	1.000
36	18	18	1.000

Table 3.8: Power to detect trend in the binomial probability for **hatchlings** for non-core sites only

Number of non-core sites surveyed annually	Revisit design	Power to detect a 50% decrease after 10 consecutive survey years
3	[1-0]	0.875
6	[1-0]	0.957
9	[1-0]	1.000
12	[1-0]	1.000

Table 3.9: Power to detect trend in the binomial probability for **fledglings** for non-core sites only

Number of non-core sites surveyed annually	Revisit design	Power to detect a 50% decrease after 10 consecutive survey years
3	[1-0]	0.816
6	[1-0]	0.969
9	[1-0]	0.988
12	[1-0]	0.996

3.4 Conclusions

Annual surveys of 27 to 30 territories consisting of a census of the 18 core sites and 9 to 12 of the non-core sites for occupancy surveys and at least 10 occupied territories for fecundity surveys should provide power greater than 0.80 for trend detection. Stratified random sampling within the non-core subpopulation will allow inference to that subpopulation of territories. MacKenzie et al. (2006) recommend the [1-0] revisit design so that the additional variation from alternating territories in and out of the survey will not affect variance estimates and therefore the power to detect trends. However, management goals may necessitate the use of serially-alternating revisit designs so that all territories may be visited intermittently.

Gavin Emmons stated that some territorial pairs arrive in the spring rather than in the late winter, so territories designated as "occupied" for that year may actually be unoccupied early in the survey season. This would cause underestimation of detection rates. The pilot data indicate that detection probabilities are lowest in January and gradually increase over the course of the survey season (Figure 3.1). Most of these late-winter visits occur in core territories which are visited throughout the hiking and climbing season. The occupancy model used in this application applies the assumption that occupancy is consistent throughout the monitoring period. Defining the monitoring window so that this assumption is true will allow accurate and precise estimation of occupancy and detection rates. Determining the occupancy sampling time frame *a priori* will not bias the results but will provide more accurate estimation of detection and occupancy rates from a more balanced data set.

62

4. SPOTTED OWL POWER ANALYSES

The monitoring goals of the spotted owl protocol are to detect substantial long-term trends in spotted owl occupancy and fecundity rates at activity sites within NPS boundaries in Marin County, California. The methods described in Section 2 are used to calculate the power to detect trend in spotted owl metrics. Some background on the sampling design is followed by discussions of the power to detect trend in spotted owl occupancy and fecundity rates. For a Type I error rate of 0.2, the power to detect declines of 4%, 10%, 12%, and 15% in each indicator of interest over 5- and 10-year periods in a one-sided alternative hypothesis is examined for several sample sizes of sites and revisit designs. Results from an initial analysis provide the basis for further power analysis to inform survey design choices.

4.1 Sampling design

The spotted owl study area consists of all federal lands within Marin County and includes Golden Gate National Recreation Area, Muir Woods National Monument, Point Reyes National Seashore, and Samuel P. Taylor State Park, as well as a 400m buffer around these parks. The sampling frame consists of all sites within the study area where a spotted owl has been observed in any survey conducted between 1997 and 2006. A total of 66 sites were initially identified from this list. Eight sites were removed due to inaccessibility (on private land or unsafe to access) or close proximity to another site. Two sites were added to the frame that fell just outside of the GIS buffer. The final 60 sites serve as the sampling frame for occupancy monitoring. Occupancy surveys are conducted between March 1 and August 31.

Between March 1 and May 31, nesting status is assessed. From May 1 to August 31, nests are monitored and fecundity measurements are collected. Fecundity surveys are only conducted at sites containing territorial females, including resident single females and both nesting and non-nesting pairs. Sites that do not meet these criteria of a territorial female are omitted from fecundity estimation based on a "non-target" assessment. Inclusion probabilities may be adjusted to account for changes in the sampling frame so that unbiased estimation is achieved. The number of locations monitored for fecundity is given for the pilot data collected from 1999 to 2008 (Table 4.1). For fecundity monitoring, the subset of 48 sites containing a nesting pair during at least one year is used as the sampling frame.

Since fecundity measurements are conditional on territorial female at a monitored territory, the target population can change from year to year. Furthermore, locations that had not previously hosted a territorial female could later be colonized, thus meeting the definition of the target population for fecundity monitoring. Unfortunately, some nests cannot be evaluated for occupancy by territorial females until later in the survey season, so selecting a sample from the set of sites meeting the criteria for fecundity sampling is not possible. Therefore, a random sample from the sampling frame of 48 sites will be used for monitoring. The fecundity sample should be larger than necessary given that roughly 70% of the sites are eligible for fecundity surveys (David Press, personal communication).

Table 4.1: Number of locations sampled for SPOW fecundity monitoring by year

Year	Number of locations	Number of fecundity locations
1999	34	19
2000	34	25
2001	34	25
2002	41	27
2003	34	28
2004	24	24
2005	21	21
2006	NA	NA
2007	25	12
2008	25	12
2009	30	26

One of six possible occupancy status categories is assigned for each location each year (Table 4.2). These occupancy categories are mutually exclusive, with all locations falling into only one category each year. Ultimately, the most appropriate occupancy model would estimate occupancy trends for all status categories simultaneously so that the sum of occupancy estimates across categories is always one. However, the available literature has not incorporated techniques for estimating occupancy for more than two categories with methods for trend estimation. Given the instability of occupancy and detection models in the univariate case (discussed in the next section), the multivariate case was not explored.

Table 4.2: Occupancy categories

Occupancy code	Description
PR	Resident pair detected
PU	Pair detected but pair occupancy not confirmed
RS	Resident single
SU	Resident single detected but occupancy not confirmed
UK	Occupancy status unknown
UO	Unoccupied

To estimate occupancy according to the SFAN definition of occupancy, only detections verifying territorial behavior are used. The proportion of detections falling within each status category is provided in Table 4.3. The majority of detections occurred within locations with a resident pair. Resident single occupancy is rare in comparison. Status categories for which territoriality is unknown (PU, SU, and UK) also occur less frequently. Without adjusting for imperfect detection, observed detection rates imply high occupancy rates for resident pairs. However, some of the categories are quite rare and estimates of the binomial probabilities may be unstable because they are close to 0 (Olkin, et al., 1981).

Table 4.3: Observed status category frequency among all detections by year

Year	PR	PU	RS	SU	UK	UO
1999	0.82	0.03	0.03	0.03	0.02	0.06
2000	0.81	0.00	0.05	0.04	0.01	0.09
2001	0.85	0.00	0.02	0.00	0.01	0.13
2002	0.89	0.00	0.04	0.02	0.00	0.05
2003	0.96	0.01	0.00	0.00	0.01	0.02
2004	0.92	0.00	0.05	0.00	0.02	0.01
2005	0.88	0.00	0.04	0.00	0.04	0.03
2006	0.67	0.00	0.16	0.11	0.05	0.02
2007	0.79	0.07	0.06	0.04	0.00	0.04
2008	0.79	0.02	0.04	0.07	0.01	0.08

4.2 Occupancy analysis

The pilot data for occupancy modeling are taken from the set of sites chosen for monitoring. Sites outside the SFAN monitoring area were excluded because they do not represent the target population for which trends will be estimated. Covariate information available for occupancy and detection modeling is described in Table 4.4. These variables represent all modeling variables included by SFAN personnel in the pilot data set.

Table 4.4: Covariate information available for occupancy and detection modeling

Covariate code	Description
Year	Year of the survey
Month	Month of the survey
Barred	Indicator of barred owl detection at a site for a given year
Daytime	Indicator that survey occurred during the day
Call	Indicator that a call method was used
ObsNum	Number of observers present during the survey

The process of model selection was problematic for the spotted owl pilot data. Because occupancy analysis is based on a nonlinear model, obtaining a positive-definite Hessian matrix was not possible for some models. The Hessian matrix affects the estimates of variance for occupancy and detection regression parameter estimates which affects trend testing. Model selection was conducted using AIC as the model selection criterion (Bayes Information Criterion was also examined but selected similar models). However, models chosen with AIC often did not provide positive-definite Hessian matrices. The model with the lowest AIC and a positive-definite Hessian matrix was used in the power analysis for trend testing. The final occupancy and detection models selected with this approach are provided for each status category in Table 4.5. The final models were often a reduced version of the model with the lowest AIC indicating that simpler models are more stable for occupancy estimation.

The occupancy estimates by category are provided in Table 4.6. For each status category, occupancy estimates are provided either for the model including the indicator of barred owl presence (estimates of occupancy with and without barred owl presence are provided in the second and third columns) or the model without a factor for barred owl presence (occupancy estimates given in the fourth column). Columns for the unused model contain a "-" to indicate that this model was not used. Due to the complexities of estimating trend with a multi-category occupancy classification, a univariate approach was used and occupancy estimates do not sum to 1. Notice that the presence of barred owls in a site and year decreases pair occupancy but increases the single-unknown and unoccupied status categories. This result suggests that the effect of barred owl presence is to reduce pair occupancy and inhibit territorial behavior as evidenced by the positive effects observed in the SU and UK status categories.

Table 4.5: Final occupancy and detection models for each spotted owl occupancy category

Status category	Occupancy model $\log\left(\dfrac{\pi_{ij}}{1-\pi_{ij}}\right)$	Detection model $\log\left(\dfrac{p_{ij}}{1-p_{ij}}\right)$
PR	$\gamma_0 + \gamma_1 \text{Barred}_{ij}$	$\beta_0 + \beta_1 \text{Day}_{ij} + \beta_2 \text{Call}_{ij} + \beta_3 \text{ObsNum}_{ij}$
PU	γ_0	$\beta_0 + \beta_1 \text{Day}_{ij} + \beta_2 \text{Call}_{ij}$
RS	γ_0	$\beta_0 + \beta_1 \text{Day}_{ij} + \beta_2 \text{Call}_{ij}$
SU	$\gamma_0 + \gamma_1 \text{Barred}_{ij}$	$\beta_0 + \beta_1 \text{Day}_{ij} + \beta_2 \text{Call}_{ij}$
UK	γ_0	$\beta_0 + \beta_1 \text{Month}_{ij} + \beta_2 \text{Call}_{ij}$
UO	$\gamma_0 + \gamma_1 \text{Barred}_{ij}$	$\beta_0 + \beta_1 \text{Call}_{ij}$

Table 4.6: Occupancy estimates (and standard errors) from the final model for each spotted owl occupancy category

Status category	Est. occupancy rate for sites with barred owls (SE)	Est. occupancy rate for sites without barred owls (SE)	Est. occupancy rate (SE)
PR	0.9197 (0.0505)	~ 1.000 (0.00001)	-
PU	-	-	0.0301 (0.0146)
RS	-	-	0.1614 (0.0428)
SU	0.2562 (0.0960)	0.1127 (0.0384)	-
UK	-	-	0.0208 (0.0058)
UO	0.1172 (0.0371)	0.0601 (0.0124)	-

Fixed and random effects for location were examined in the modeling effort for occupancy and detection rates. Adding a fixed effect for location prohibitively reduced the number of degrees of freedom available for error estimation. Modeling the location effect as a random effect in the detection model produces the heterogeneous detection probability model which is often difficult to implement in a maximum likelihood approach (MacKenzie et al. 2006). In practice, this approach resulted in site-by-year level occupancy estimates very near 1 and with nearly zero variation and corresponding detection probabilities very near zero. Incorporating the random effect into the occupancy model produced similar problems. A Bayesian approach may be more appropriate for a random effects modeling approach (MacKenzie et al. 2006).

The benefit of incorporating a fixed or random effect for location is that repeat visits to the same locations over time can reduce variance and provide more accurate trend estimation. Without a location effect, the data are treated like random samples taken independently each year (a [1-n] revisit design). MacKenzie et al. (2006) argue that the [1-0] revisit design is best for trend estimation because the models cannot distinguish between variation among different locations and that observed over time. However, the implicit occupancy model used in this analysis does not require that the same sites are visited annually because the local extinction and colonization parameters are not explicitly estimated. MacKenzie et al. (2006) recommend that the [1-0] revisit design be used unless destructive sampling occurs. However, the needs of the monitoring program may dictate that all sites be visited periodically, making a revisit design that accommodates those requirements more desirable.

The revisit designs initially under consideration were the [1-0], [2-2], [(1-0)^5,(2-2)], and [(1-0)^{10},(2-2)] designs (Figures 4.1 – 4.4, respectively, are provided for a set annual sample of 40 sites). The difference in the latter two designs is that an annual panel of 5 sites is used in the [(1-0)^5,(2-2)] design while an annual panel of 10 sites is used in the [(1-0)^{10},(2-2)] design. As discussed, the trend analysis treats the data as if a [1-n] design has been used. The [1-n] revisit design has the lowest power for trend detection and therefore provides conservative power results. The replication within a location cannot be used to induce a correlation within a location over time to reduce the variance of the trend estimate. The results of the power analysis for the six spotted owl occupancy status categories, monitoring periods of 5 and 10 years, and all revisit designs are provided in Appendix A. Power is given for a one-sided hypothesis test of no change versus a decreasing trend over time. The results of the initial power analysis demonstrate that the revisit designs are indistinguishable when neither the occupancy nor the detection model includes an effect for location.

The detection model exhibited considerable influence on the final estimates of occupancy. Estimated occupancy could vary widely depending on what covariates were included in the detection model. The problems described above indicate that detection models might perform best when they are simple and covariates uncorrelated with predictors used in both the occupancy and detection models are used.

Year

Panel	1	2	3	4	5	6	7	8
1	40	40	40	40	40	40	40	40
ANNUAL TOTAL	40	40	40	40	40	40	40	40

Figure 4.1: [1-0] revisit design for an annual sample of 40 sites

Year

Panel	1	2	3	4	5	6	7	8
1	40	40			40	40		
ANNUAL TOTAL	40	40	0	0	40	40	0	0

Figure 4.2: [(2-2)] revisit design for an annual sample of 40 sites

Year

Panel	1	2	3	4	5	6	7	8
1	5	5	5	5	5	5	5	5
2	35	35			35	35		
ANNUAL TOTAL	40	40	5	5	40	40	5	5

Figure 4.3: $[(1\text{-}0)^5, (2\text{-}2)]$ revisit design for an annual sample of 40 sites

Year

Panel	1	2	3	4	5	6	7	8
1	10	10	10	10	10	10	10	10
2	30	30			30	30		
ANNUAL TOTAL	40	40	10	10	40	40	10	10

Figure 4.4: $[(1\text{-}0)^{10}, (2\text{-}2)]$ revisit design for an annual sample of 40 sites

Power to detect trends in pair occupancy over time (Figures A.1 and A.2) is nearly 1 for trends over either 5 or 10 years. For pairs whose occupancy status is unknown (Figures A.3 and A.4), power is considerably lower, only reaching 0.8 for annual declines of over 10% and censuses over 10 consecutive years. Power to detect declines in resident single occupancy within 5 years is below 0.8 unless all of the sites in the population are visited and declines are at least 15% annually (Figure A.5). However, the power to detect trend in resident single status is at or above 0.8 for annual samples of as few as 20 locations per year when the annual decline is 10% or greater over 10 years (Figure A.6). Power for trend detection within 5 years is consistently below 0.8 for the single unknown, unknown, and unoccupied categories, but power to detect trends within 10 years are near 0.8 for the single unknown and unoccupied categories when declines are at least 10% annually.

Overall, the power to detect trend in pair occupancy is excellent at the $\alpha = 0.2$ level. However, higher levels of effort or change are required for trend detection in other status categories because of their relative rarity. Maximum likelihood estimates of binomial probabilities that are close to 0 are generally unstable (Olkin et al., 1981). This may explain the decrease in power for an increasing number of sites in the power plot of unoccupied status (Figure 4.16).

Based on the results of the initial power analysis, the spotted owl workgroup determined that monitoring the occupancy of spotted owl pairs is of greatest importance. The relative rarity of the other status categories causes trend estimation to be more difficult unless changes are extreme. Data collection will continue for the other status categories so that baseline information is available for monitoring any future changes, but trends will only be calculated for spotted owl pairs.

In addition to focusing inference on the occupancy of spotted owl pairs, the results of the initial occupancy power analysis indicated that power to detect trend was adequate for a 5-year monitoring period. The final sampling design for occupancy and fecundity sampling needed to meet some additional criteria, including visiting all occupancy and fecundity sites at least once within one revisit cycle, obtaining an adequate fecundity sample size given that about 70% of occupancy sites are eligible for fecundity surveys, and possible restrictions on annual funding. Two possible funding scenarios were proposed: annual funding and funding for two consecutive year of high survey intensity followed by two years with low survey intensity. Based on these two funding scenarios and two proposed sample sizes from the fecundity analysis, four revisit designs were examined (Figures 4.5 to 4.8).

The four proposed revisit designs provide options for sampling designs given different levels and cycles of funding and for annual samples of 35 and 43 locations so that 25 and 30 fecundity sites may be visited in fully-funded years. The revisit design notation $(1-3)^{1/2}$ indicates that only half of the [1-3] panels are visited, so there are two [1-3] panels visited and no sites from this revisit design are surveyed in the other two years.

Panel	Revisit design	1	2	3	4	5	6	7	8
	Year								
1	[1-0]	15	15	15	15	15	15	15	15
2	[1-3]	20				20			
3	[1-3]		20				20		
ANNUAL TOTAL		35	35	15	15	35	35	15	15

Figure 4.5: $[(1-0)^{10}, (1-3)^{1/2}]$ revisit design for an annual sample of 35 sites

Panel	Revisit design	1	2	3	4	5	6	7	8
	Year								
1	[1-0]	26	26	26	26	26	26	26	26
2	[1-3]	17				17			
3	[1-3]		17				17		
ANNUAL TOTAL		43	43	26	26	43	43	26	26

Figure 4.6: $[(1-0)^{26}, (1-3)^{1/2}]$ revisit design for an annual sample of 43 sites

Panel	Revisit design	1	2	3	4	5	6	7	8
	Year								
1	[1-0]	28	28	28	28	28	28	28	28
2	[1-3]	8				8			
3	[1-3]		8				8		
4	[1-3]			8				8	
5	[1-3]				8				8
ANNUAL TOTAL		36	36	36	36	36	36	36	36

Figure 4.7: $[(1-0)^{28}, (1-3)]$ revisit design for an annual sample of 36 sites

Panel	Revisit design	1	2	3	4	5	6	7	8
	Year								
1	[1-0]	40	40	40	40	40	40	40	40
2	[1-3]	5				5			
3	[1-3]		5				5		
4	[1-3]			5				5	
5	[1-3]				5				5
ANNUAL TOTAL		45	45	45	45	45	45	45	45

Figure 4.8: $[(1-0)^{40}, (1-3)]$ revisit design for an annual sample of 45 sites

If location effects could be incorporated into the model, we would expect power to be lowest for the revisit design represented in Figure 1 and the highest for Figure 4 based on the increasing size of the annual revisit panel. The [1-0] annual panel sites will be selected from the list of sites that fall in both the occupancy and fecundity sampling frames. Then the remaining sites could be

70

ordered randomly and allotted to the other panels. If needed, the sites included in both the occupancy and fecundity frames could be balanced among years in the remaining panels, thus also balancing the sites that historically have not contained successful nests.

The power for each revisit design is provided in Table 4.7. The power to detect trend is very high because the estimated occupancy rate is near 1, making declines easy to detect. Power was estimated to be near or equal to one for all revisit scenarios and both levels of change given a Type II error of 0.20, so power was also examined at the $\alpha = 0.10$ level. At this level, power is at or above 0.98 for all revisit designs. Because site-level effects are not incorporated in this occupancy analysis, power is conservative for trend detection. Furthermore, power calculated from this model is a function of the total sample size rather than of panel sample sizes.

Table 4.7: Power to detect trends in spotted owl pair occupancy within five consecutive survey years for four revisit designs

Revisit design	Power to detect a 4% annual decrease in occupancy		Power to detect a 10% annual decrease in occupancy	
	$\alpha = 0.10$	$\alpha = 0.20$	$\alpha = 0.10$	$\alpha = 0.20$
$[(1-0)^{15}, (1-3)^{1/2}]$	0.992	1.000	1.000	1.000
$[(1-0)^{26}, (1-3)^{1/2}]$	0.992	1.000	1.000	1.000
$[(1-0)^{28}, (1-3)]$	0.992	1.000	1.000	1.000
$[(1-0)^{40}, (1-3)]$	0.996	1.000	1.000	1.000

4.3 Fecundity analysis

Fecundity of spotted owls is measured by the number of fledglings per territorial female. Nesting spotted owls can produce 0 to 3 fledglings, though a maximum of two fledglings was observed from the pilot data. The 1998-2008 pilot data indicate that zero inflation may be an issue (Figure 4.5). Zero inflation may result from a high number of non-nesting pairs or nest failures related to predation or environmental factors.

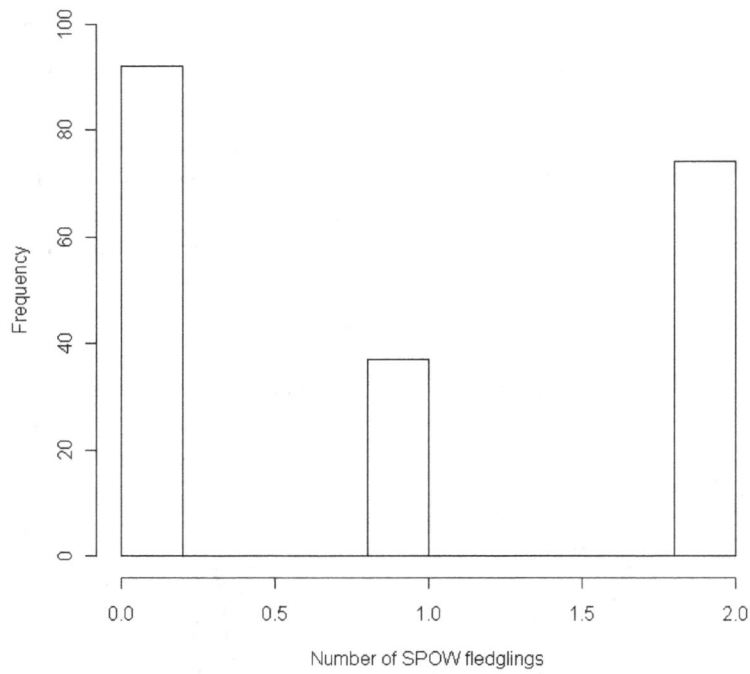

Figure 4.5: Histogram of detected spotted owl fledglings across sites and years from the pilot data

Fecundity is measured as the binomial probability for fledglings. These estimates are provided in Table 4.8 by year. While the estimates indicate an increasing trend (Figure 4.6), the increase is not significant (LRT test statistic: 0.0043, p-value: 0.9479). The probability of not detecting an extra zero is estimated as 0.6395 (SE 0.0466).

Table 4.8: Estimated binomial probabilities for fledgling

Year	Estimated binomial probability for fledglings (SE)
1999	0.4715 (0.0686)
2000	0.4724 (0.0574)
2001	0.4732 (0.0473)
2002	0.4741 (0.0393)
2003	0.4750 (0.0349)
2004	0.4758 (0.0353)
2005	0.4767 (0.0405)
2006	0.4776 (0.0490)
2007	0.4784 (0.0593)
2008	0.4793 (0.0707)

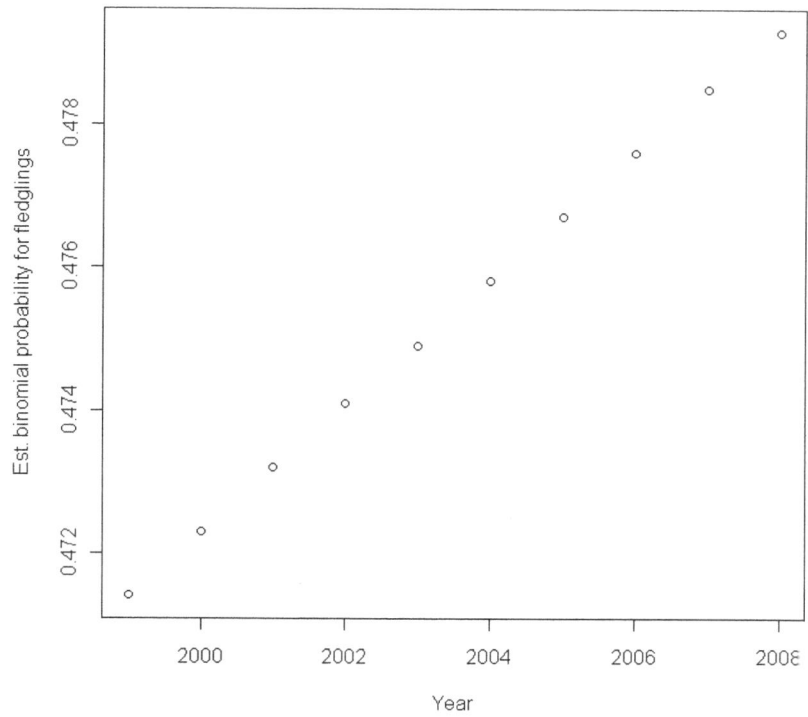

Figure 4.6: Estimated binomial probabilities for spotted owl fledglings by year

The power to detect trends in fledgling rates is calculated as described in section 2.2. The intercept-only model for zero-inflation is constant across all locations and years. The fledgling rate model is allowed to change linearly across years for trend testing. The power to detect decreasing trends in spotted owl fecundity is based on the likelihood ratio test for monitoring periods of 5 years (Figure 4.7) and 10 years (Figure 4.8). Twenty to 25 locations with resident females must be surveyed annually to detect decreasing trends of at least 10% within 5 years. Power to detect a 4% decline within 5 years never exceeds 0.5. For a 10-year monitoring period, power to detect decreasing trends of at least 10% is at least 0.8 for samples as low as 10 occupied locations per year. Around 30 nests must be visited annually to detect a 4% decline with power of 0.8 within 10 years. Out of 25 sites selected for fecundity monitoring, the 2007 and 2008 surveys resulted in 12 sites with territorial females for fecundity analysis. At this level of effort, longer monitoring time frames are required to achieve adequate power for trend detection.

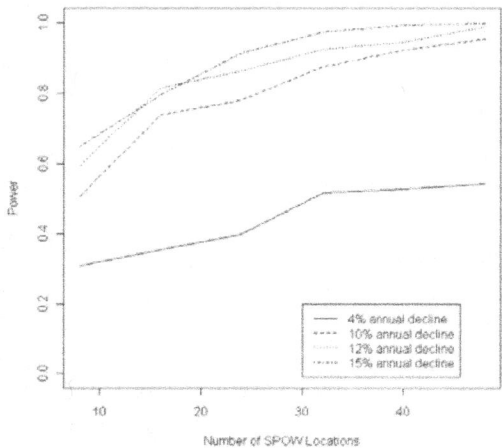

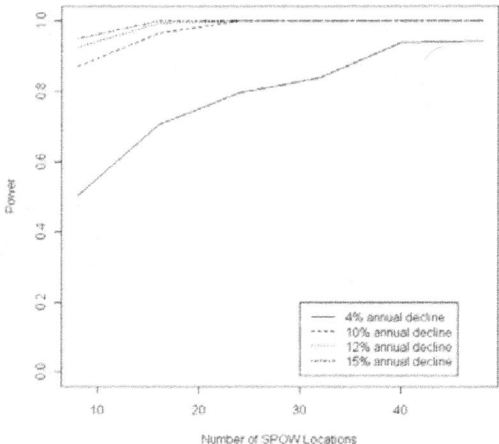

Figure 4.7: Power to detect trend in the binomial probability of spotted owl hatchling success in 5 consecutive survey years for four rates of change

Figure 4.8: Power to detect trend in the binomial probability of spotted owl hatchling success in 10 consecutive survey years for four rates of change

4.4 Conclusions

The power to detect decreasing trends in spotted owl occupancy is nearly 1 for the pair occupancy status. Power to detect declines in sites with resident singles, sites with single spotted owls with unknown status, and in unoccupied sites exceeds 0.8 when annual declines are at least 10% for monitoring of at least 10 years. Power to detect trends in the pair unknown and unknown categories is uniformly low based on the rarity of these status categories.

The power to detect trends in spotted owl fecundity within 5 years is at least 0.8 when the annual decline is at least 10% and at least 25 to 30 sites with known reproductive outcomes are visited annually. Given that roughly 70% of the sites visited qualify for fecundity monitoring, an initial sample of 35 to 43 sites is needed to obtain the desired sample size. For a 10-year monitoring window, power is around 0.9 even for annual fecundity samples as small as 10 territories when annual declines are at least 10%. When the annual decline is 4% over 10 years, at least 30 territories must be surveyed annually to achieve power of 0.8 or more.

5. CONCLUSIONS

Overall, power for trend detection is high for prairie falcon and spotted owl monitoring. For prairie falcon monitoring, 27 to 30 (18 core and 9 to 12 non-core) territories should be visited annually to achieve power of 0.8 to detect a net decline in pair occupancy of 50% in 10 years. Power to detect a similar trend in fecundity measures may be obtained by monitoring fecundity in at least 10 pair-occupied sites.

A preliminary power analysis indicated that power to detect trends in spotted owl pairs exceeds 0.9 at the $\alpha = 0.2$ level. Because other status categories were relatively rare and power for trend detection was low, these categories will be tracked over time but not monitored for trend. Four possible revisit designs at various levels of effort in a five-year period are proposed, each provided power of about 1.00 for trend detection in pair occupancy at the $\alpha = 0.2$ level.

The power analysis was ultimately based on a [1-n] design because a fixed or random site effect could not be incorporated into the zero-inflated binomial models. Therefore, the benefits of sampling the same sites through time could not be used to reduce the estimate of the trend variance for higher power. However, this restriction means that the power analysis is conservative. MacKenzie et al. (2006) suggest that a Bayesian analysis might resolve this problem encountered in maximum likelihood estimation. If maximum estimation is to be used to trend estimation and testing, then MacKenzie et al. (2006) recommend using a [1-0] revisit design so that additional sites do not rotate into the sample from year to year and increase site-to-site variation. This additional variation cannot be explained by the model, and the additional unexplained error reduces power to detect trend. Site-level covariates related to occupancy could be incorporated into the occupancy model to account for some site-to-site differences in occupancy.

From panel design theory, it is known that revisiting the same sites each year provides the highest power for trend detection and visiting an independent random sample each year gives the lowest power to detect trend (Urquhart and Kincaid, 1999). Skipping survey years increases the amount of time required to detect trends, but adding a panel of sites visited annually can increase the power to nearly that of the always-revisit design. Without specific information to compare revisit designs, SFAN personnel may need to rely on management needs to determine what revisit design is best. If all prairie falcon territories or spotted owl locations need to be visited in a cycle, then incorporating a revisit design that visits a majority of the same sites annually will help reduce site-to-site variation. Visiting the remaining sites with a serially-alternating revisit schedule will ensure that all sites are evaluated regularly.

6. REFERENCES

Buhl-Mortensen, L. 1996. Type II statistical errors in environmental science and the precautionary principle. Marine Pollution Bulletin 32:528-531.

Gibbs, J. P., S. Droege, and P. Eagle. 1998. Monitoring populations of plants and animals. *BioScience* 48:935–940.

Jung, B.C., Jhun, M., and Lee, J.W. (2005). Bootstrap tests for overdispersion in a Zero-Inflated Poisson Regression Model, *Biometrics* 61, 626-8.

Lyles, Robert H., Hung-Mo Lin, and John M. Williamson (2007). A practical approach to computing power for generalized linear models with nominal, count, or ordinal responses. *Statistics in Medicine* 26, 1632-48.

MacDonald, T.L. (2003). Review of environmental monitoring methods: survey designs. *Environmental Monitoring and Assessment* 85, 277-292.

MacKenzie, D.I., J.D. Nichols, J.A. Royle, K.H. Pollock, L.L. Bailey, and J.E. Hines (2006). *Occupancy Estimation and Modeling*. Academic Press: San Francisco.

Mapstone, B. D. 1995. Scalable decision rules for environmental impact studies: effect size, Type I, and Type II errors. *Ecological Applications* 5:401–410.

Olkin, L. A.J. Petkau, and J.V. Zidek (1981). A comparison of n estimators for the binomial distribution. *Journal of the American Statistical Association* 76, 637-642.

Ridout, M., J. Hinde, and C.G.B. Demetrio (2001). A score test for testing a zero-inflated Poisson regression model against a zero-inflated negative binomial alternatives. *Biometrics* 57, 219-233.

Sumathi K. and Aruna Rao K. (2009) On Estimation and Tests for Zero Inflated Regression Models, *InterStat* (on-line), August http://interstat.statjournals.net/YEAR/2009/abstracts/0908004.php

Urquhart, N.S. and T.M. Kincaid (1999). Designs for detecting trend from repeated surveys of ecological resources. *Journal of Agricultural, Biological, and Environmental Statistics* 4(4), 404-414.

APPENDIX A: Power to detect trends in spotted owl occupancy status categories by revisit design

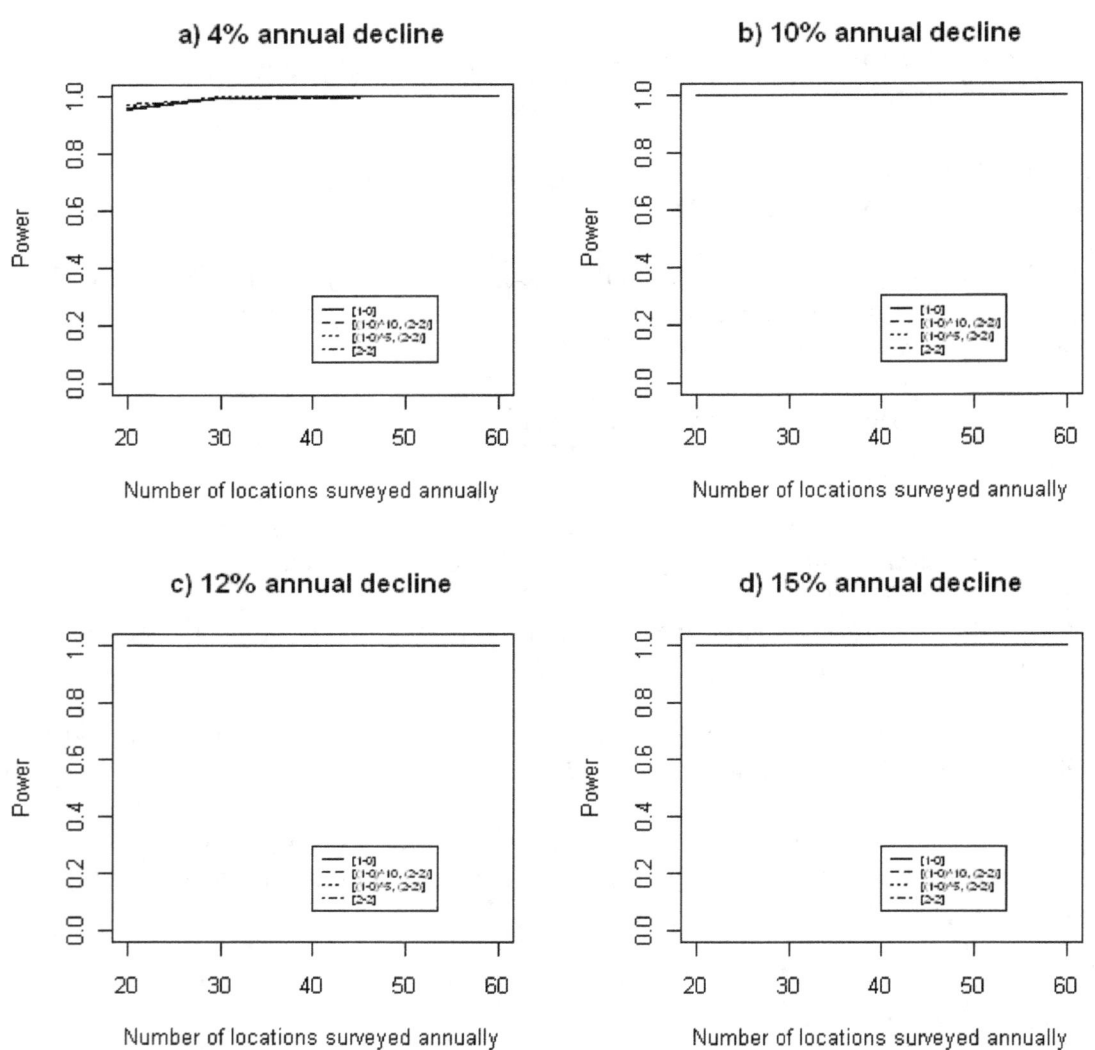

Figure A.1: Power to detect population declines in PR occupancy in tests of trend over 5 consecutive survey years for the α=0.20 significance level

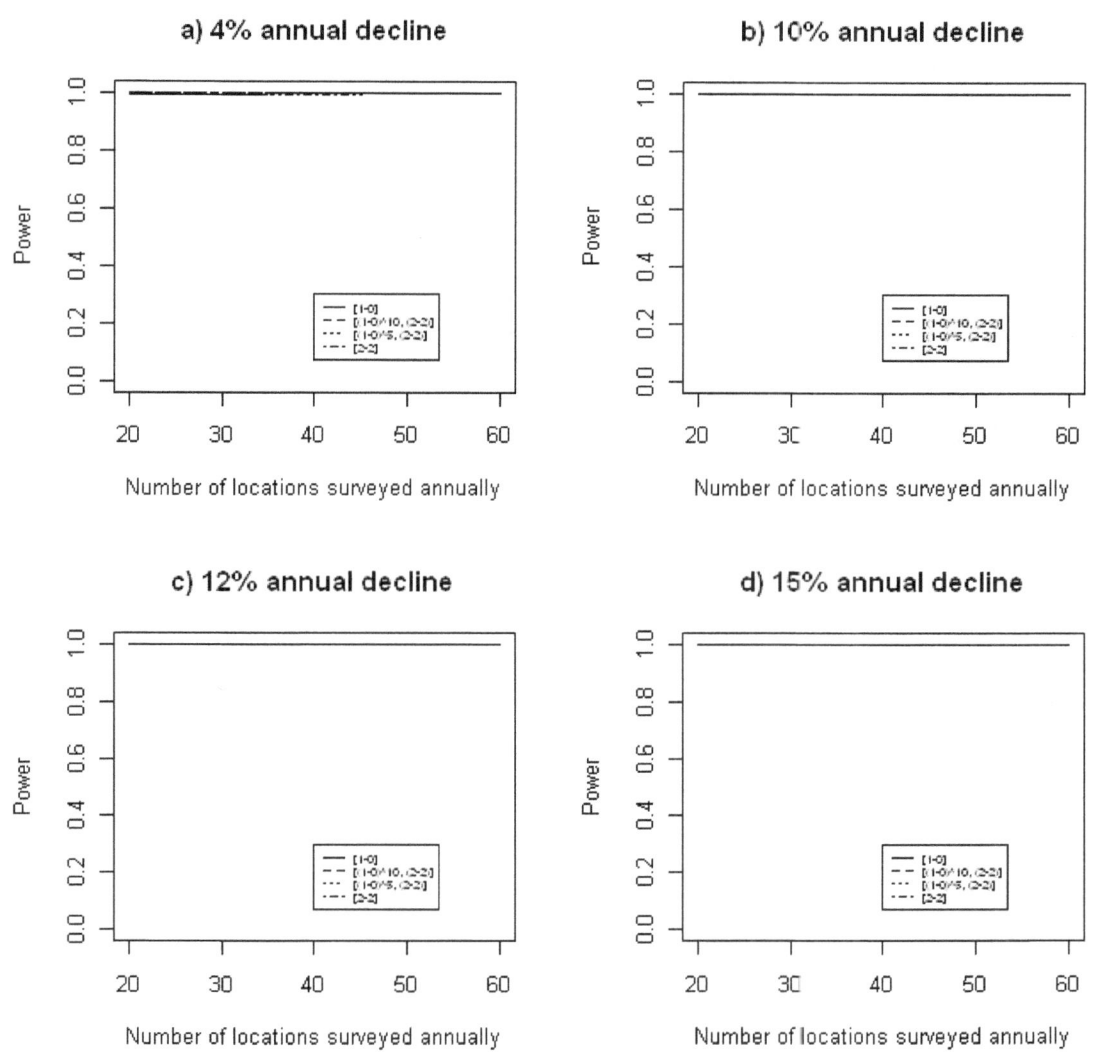

Figure A.2: Power to detect population declines in PR occupancy in tests of trend over 10 consecutive survey years for the α=0.20 significance level

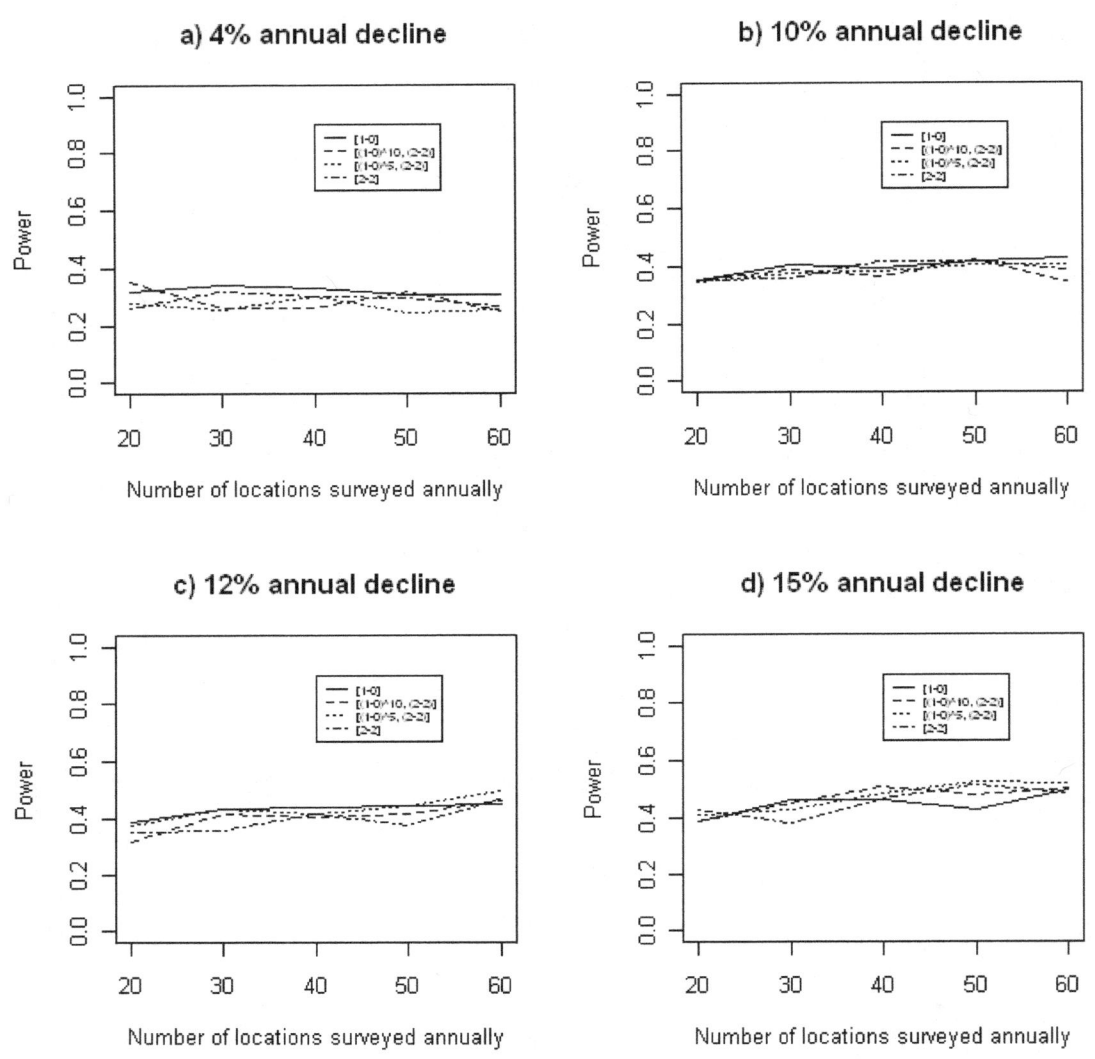

Figure A.3: Power to detect population declines in PU occupancy in tests of trend over 5 consecutive survey years for the α=0.20 significance level

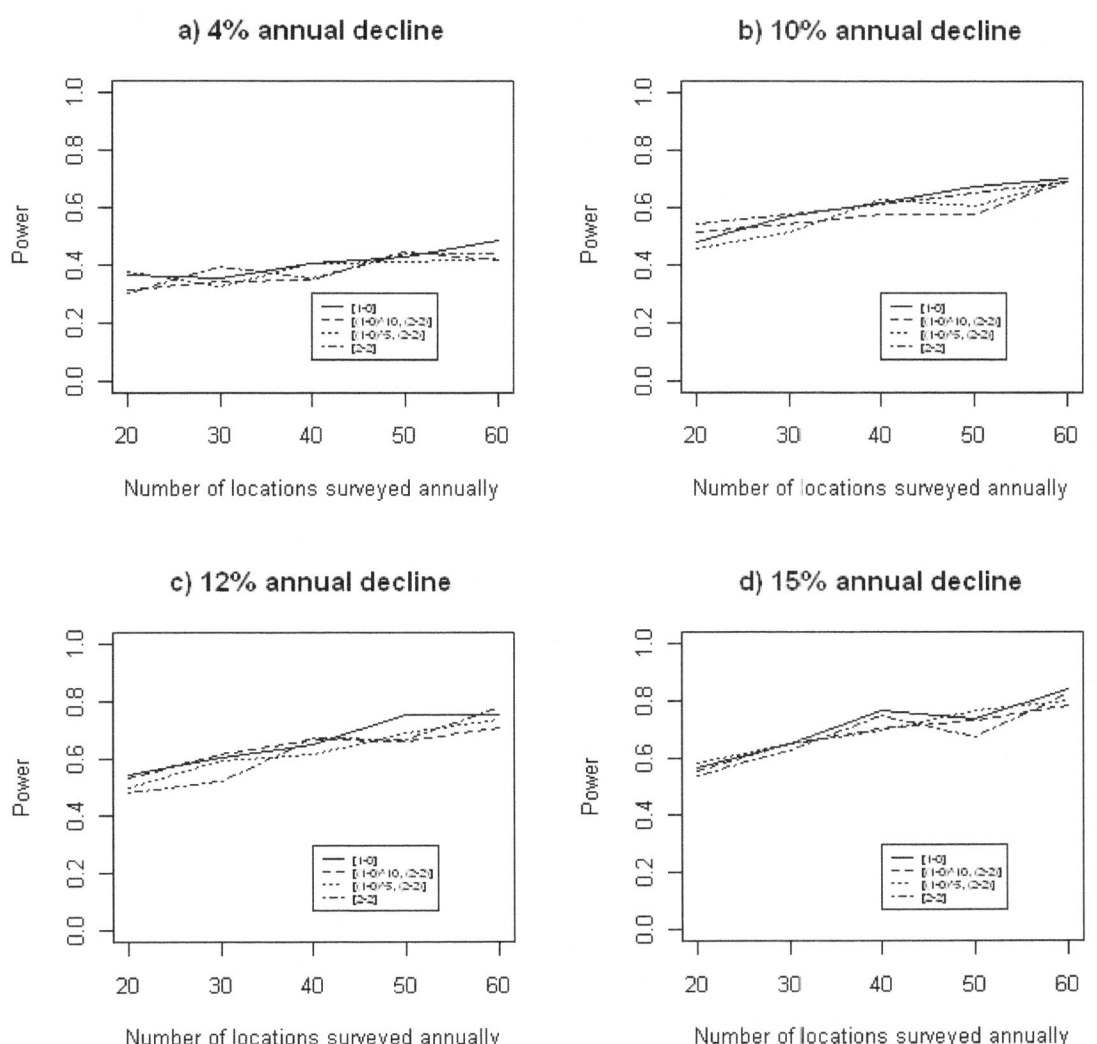

Figure A.4: Power to detect population declines in PU occupancy in tests of trend over 10 consecutive survey years for the α=0.20 significance level

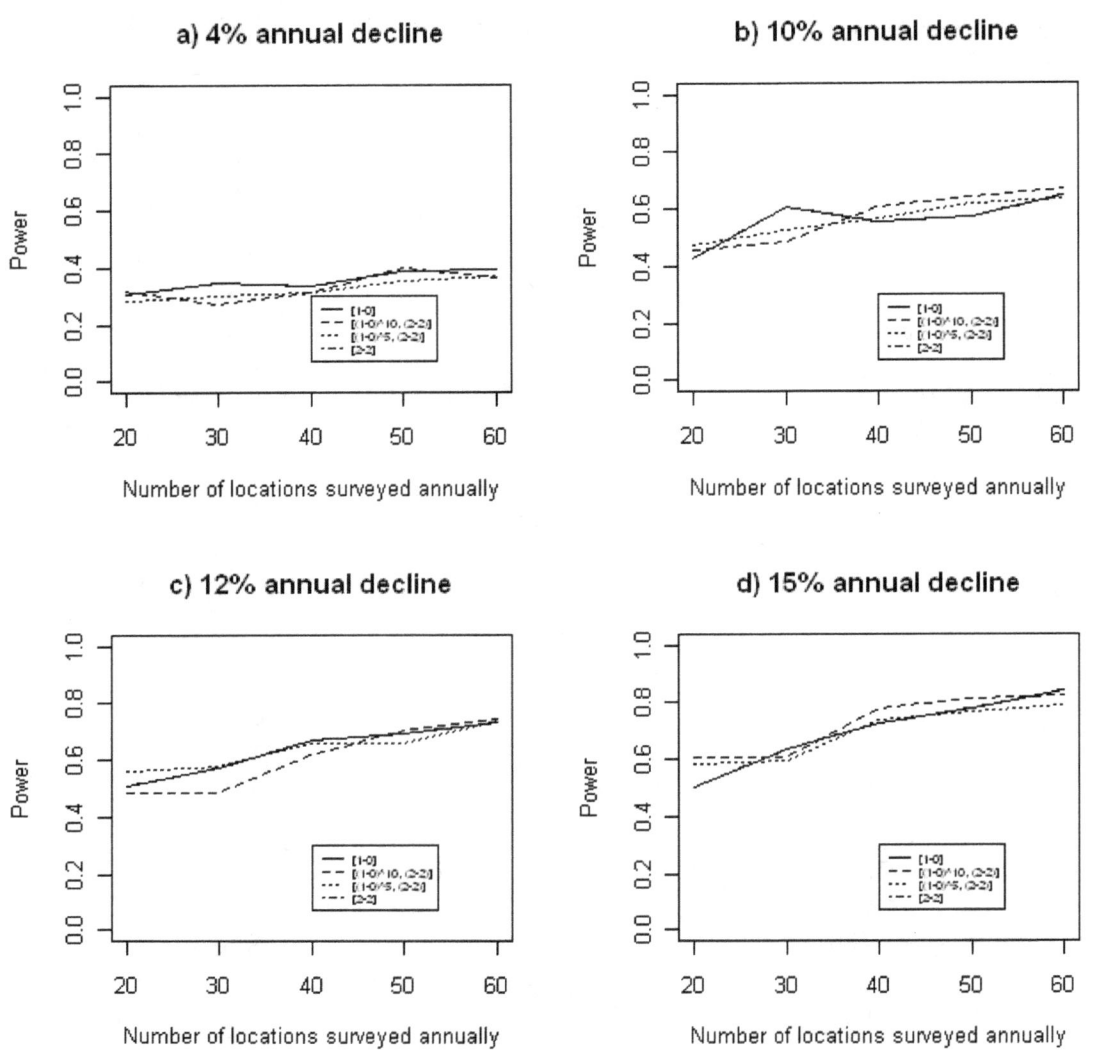

Figure A.5: Power to detect population declines in RS occupancy in tests of trend over 5 consecutive survey years for the α=0.20 significance level

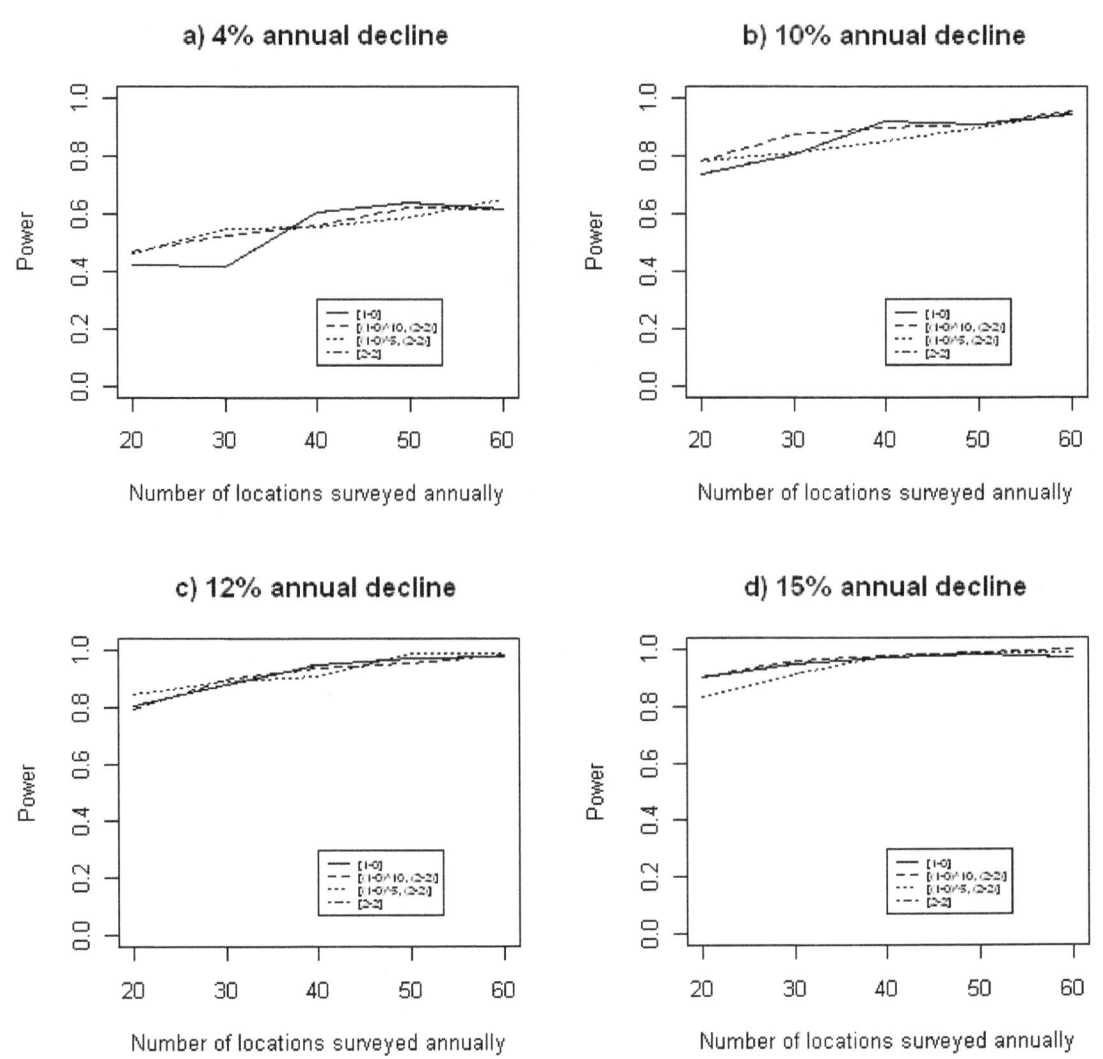

Figure A.6: Power to detect population declines in RS occupancy in tests of trend over 10 consecutive survey years for the α=0.20 significance level

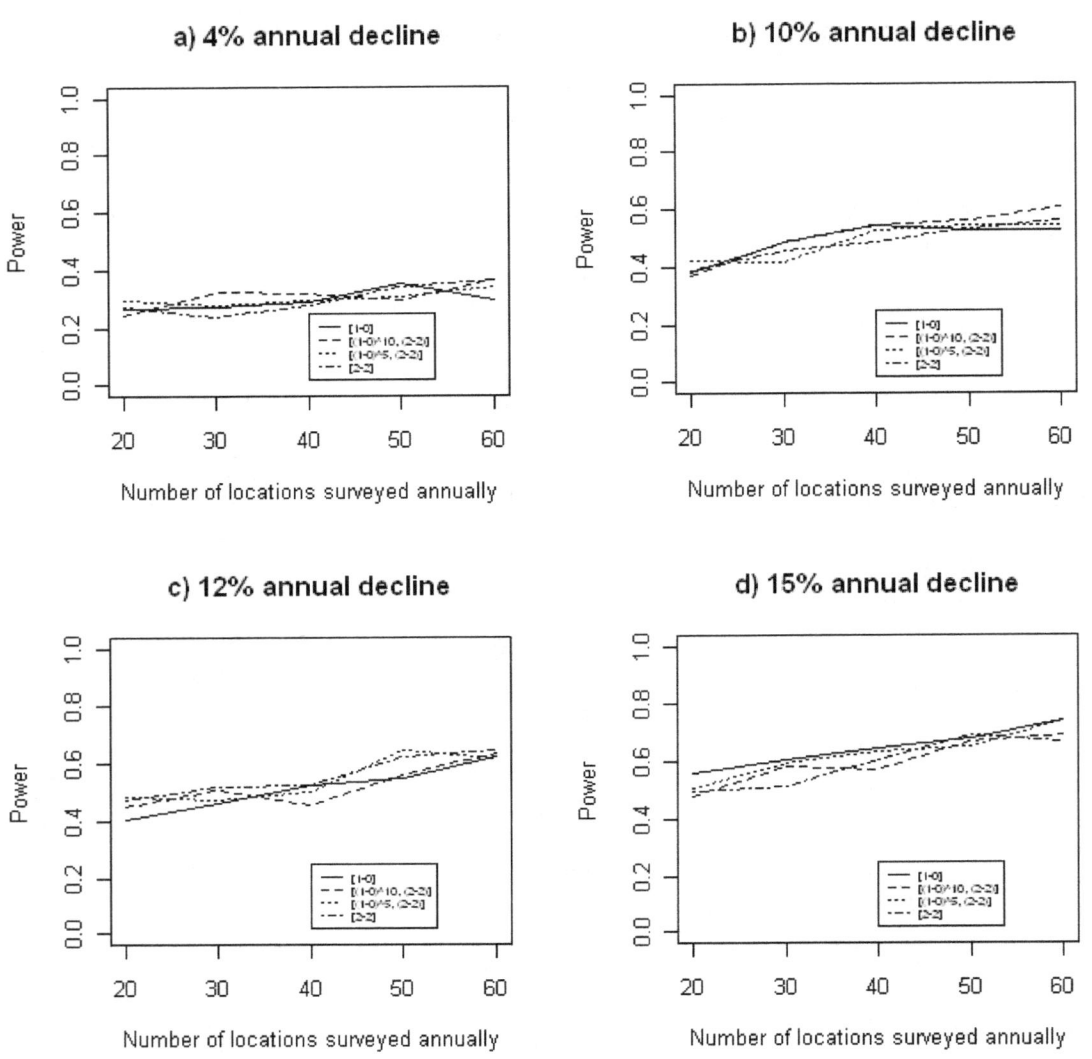

Figure A.7: Power to detect population declines in SU occupancy in tests of trend over 5 consecutive survey years for the α=0.20 significance level

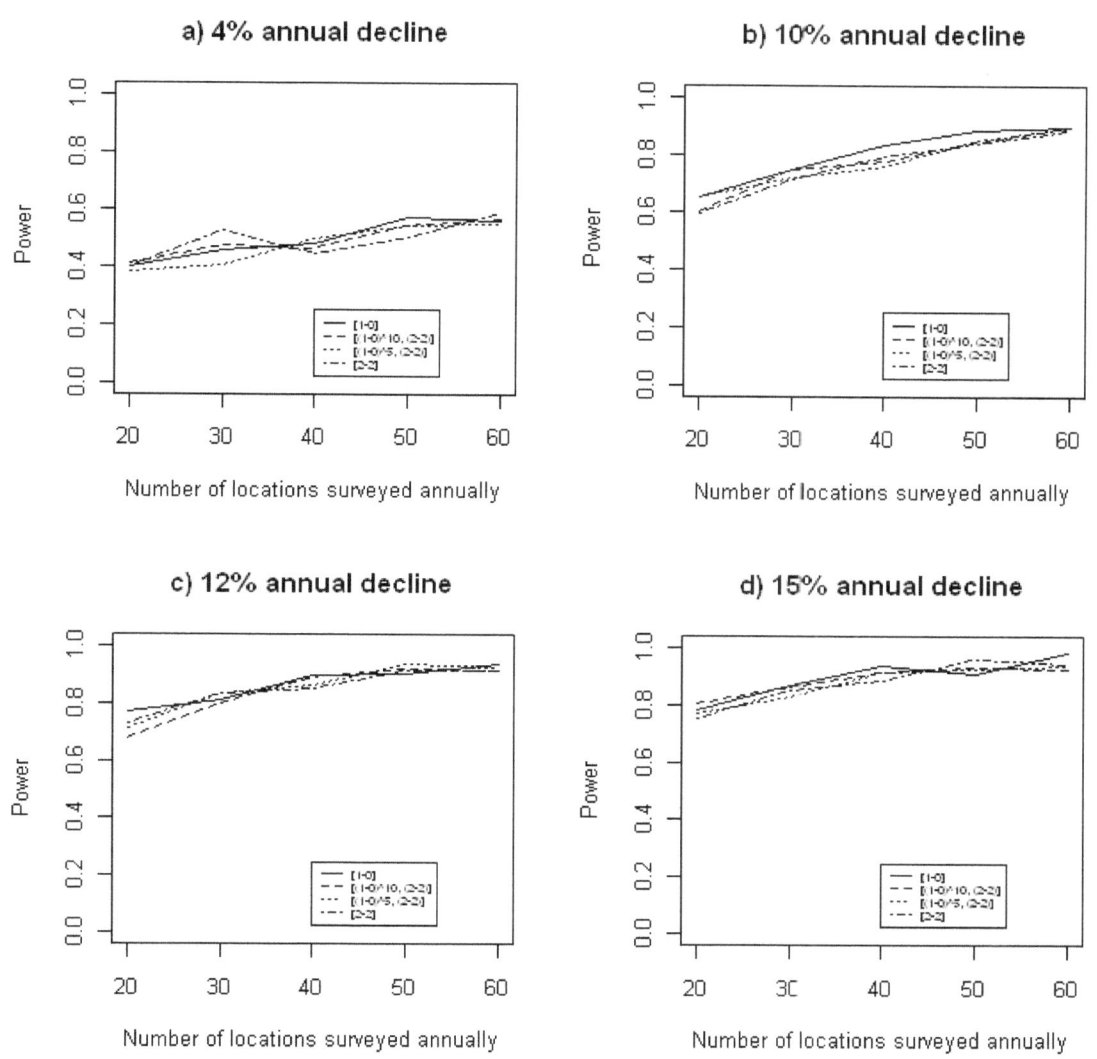

Figure A.8: Power to detect population declines in SU occupancy in tests of trend over 10 consecutive survey years for the α=0.20 significance level

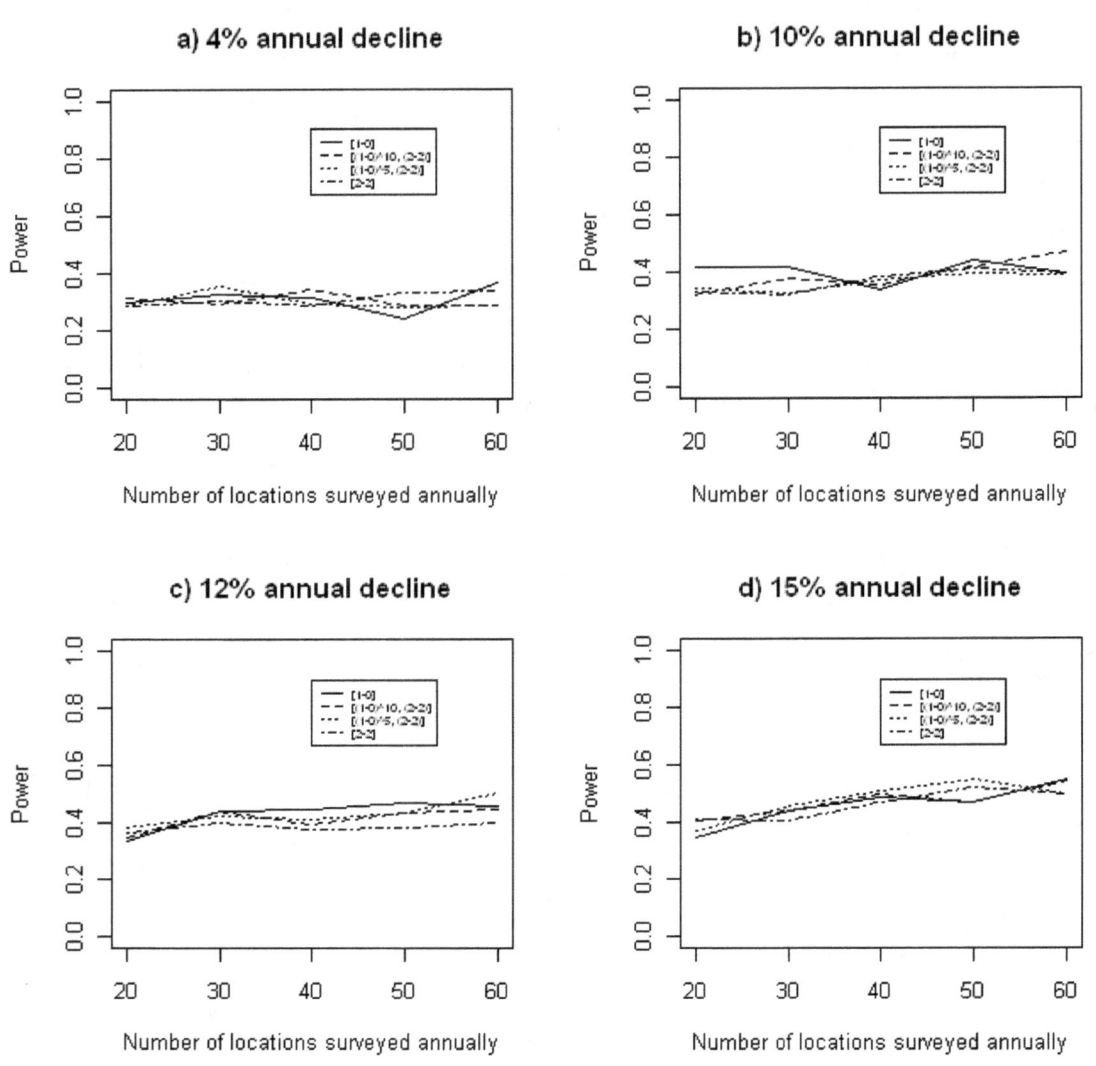

Figure A.9: Power to detect population declines in UK occupancy in tests of trend over 5 consecutive survey years for the α=0.20 significance level

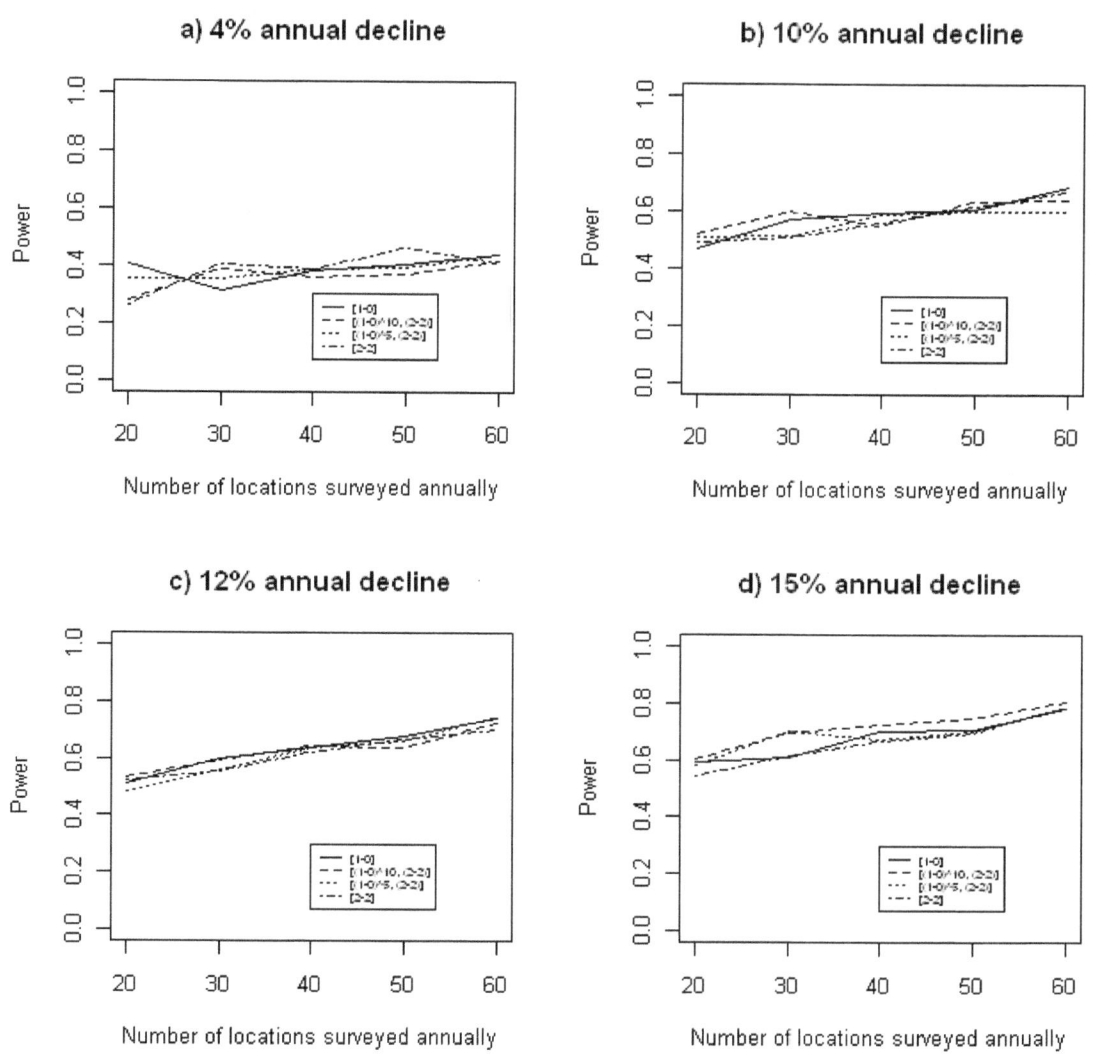

Figure A.10: Power to detect population declines in UK occupancy in tests of trend over 10 consecutive survey years for the α=0.20 significance level

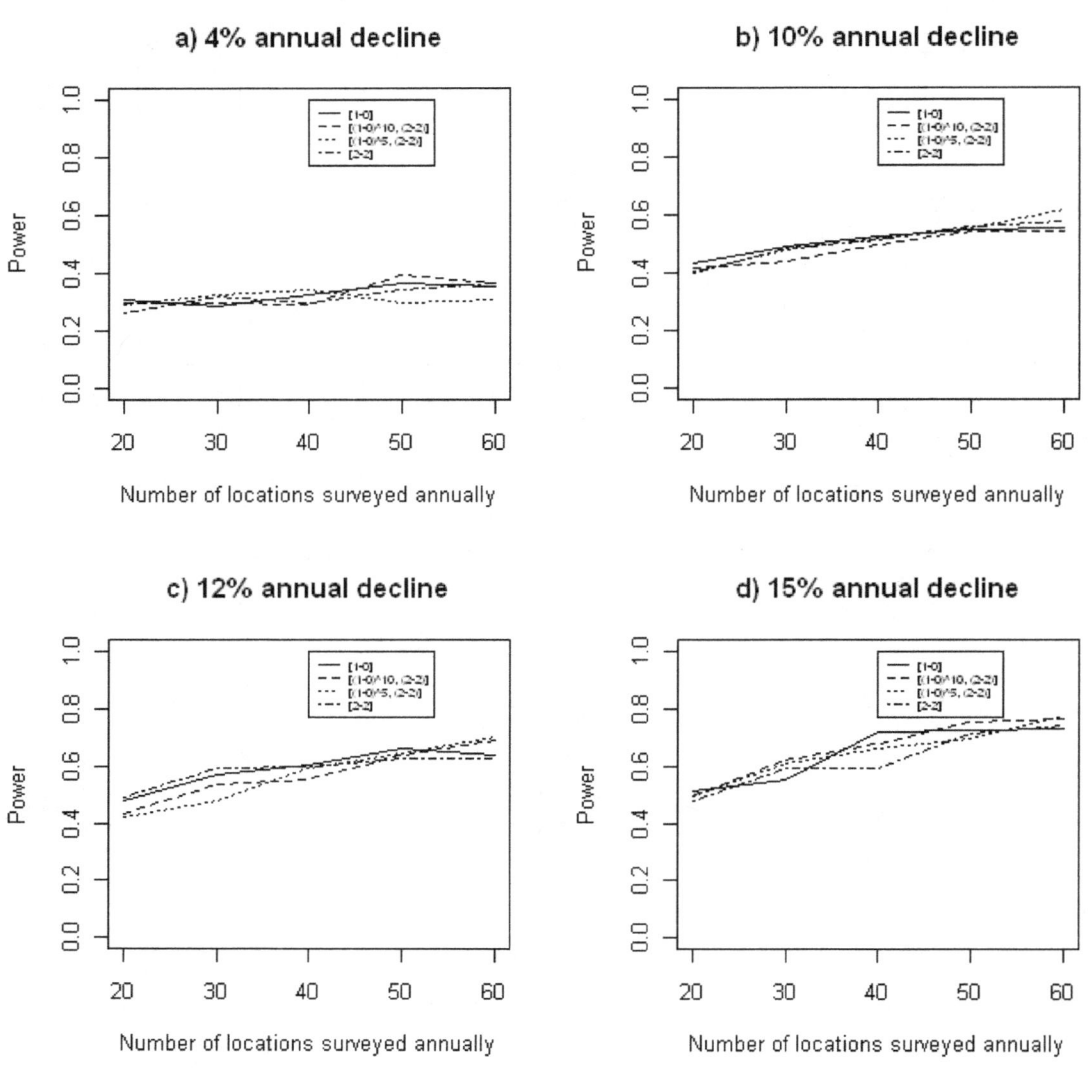

Figure A.11: Power to detect population declines in UO occupancy in tests of trend over 5 consecutive survey years for the α=0.20 significance level

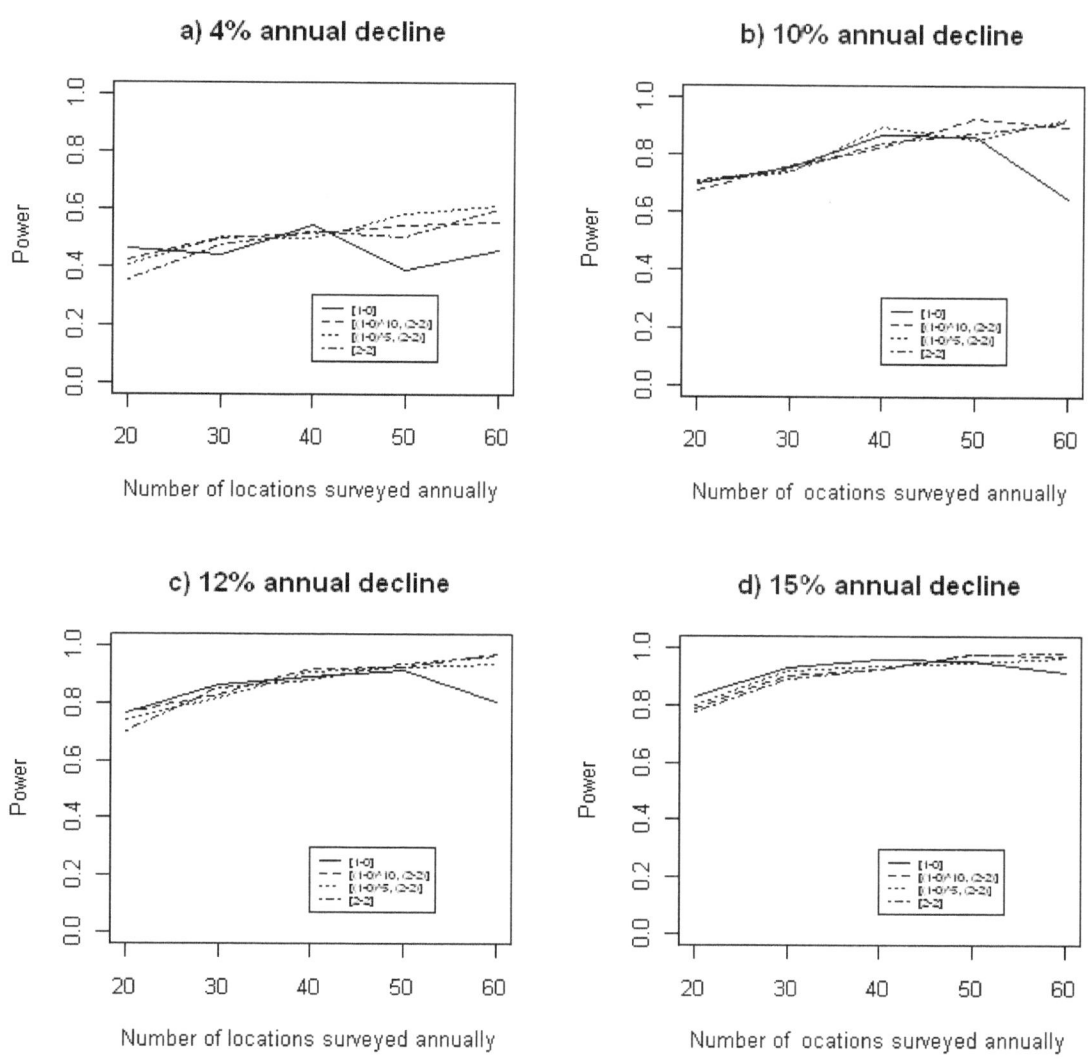

Figure A.12: Power to detect population declines in UO occupancy in tests of trend over 10 consecutive survey years for the α=0.20 significance level

Appendix B. Raptor monitoring data sheet

Date: Observer: Observation Time Start: Observation Time End: Easting: Northing: Nest Code (if nesting):	Territory: Species (and # seen): Observation Limits: Precipitation: High Temp. (F): Low Temp. (F): 0.1"Average Windspeed (mph) and Direction: Cloud Cover:

Courtship (fill in all that apply)
○ Territorial Defense (stooping, etc.):
_____

○ Display (wailing, courting flights, etc.):
_____

○ Food Exchange (prey species, times, etc.):
_____

○ Copulation (# times, start times, duration):
_____

○ Nest Site Inspections (specify sites, behavior, etc.):
_____

○ Adult Feeds Self (prey species, times, etc.):
_____

○ Sleep Roost:

Incubation (fill in all that apply and provide details)
○ Incubation (sex of adult, duration, etc.):_____
○ Nest switch (# times, etc.):_____
○ Food Drop (specify prey, male to female, times,
etc.):_____
_____

○ Adult Feeds Self (prey species, times, etc.):
_____

○ Eggs Seen (yes/no, #, etc.):

Nestlings / Fledglings (fill in all that apply and provide details)
○ Nestlings (#, age, explain aging):
_____

○ Fledglings (#, days out of nest, explain): _____
○ Food Drop (prey species, times, to adult, nestlings, or fledglings):
_____

○ Adult Feeds Self (prey species, times, etc.):
_____

○ Adult Feeds Young (prey species, times, # nestlings / fledglings
fed)_____
_____

○ Nestlings / Fledglings Feed Selves (prey species, times, # young feeding):

Photo Code _____ OR Drawing (label & detail activity):	Extra Comments:
Version 1.1 (August 2007)	

Appendix C. Raptor monitoring data sheet example

This is an example of a filled out data sheet used during the data sheet testing phase.

NPS 114/111562, November 2011